Revolutionary Rexroth

© 1964 Morgan Gibson

Revolutionary Rexroth

Poet of East-West Wisdom

Morgan Gibson

ARCHON BOOKS
1986

Composition by The Publishing Nexus Incorporated
Guilford, Connecticut

Printed in the United States of America

*The paper in this book meets the guidelines for permanence and
durability of the Committee on Production Guidelines for Book
Longevity of the Council on Library Resources.*

Library of Congress Cataloging-in-Publication Data

Gibson, Morgan, 1929–
Revolutionary Rexroth, poet of East-West wisdom.

Bibliography: p.
Includes index.
1. Rexroth, Kenneth, 1905–   —Criticism and interpretation.
2. Rexroth, Kenneth, 1905–   —Knowledge—Asia. 3. Asia in
literature. 4. East and West in literature. 5. Philosophy in literature.
6. Revolutionary poetry, American—History and criticism. I. Title
PS3535.E923Z73   1986   811'.52   86-7948
ISBN 0-208-02121-3 (alk. paper)

Contents

Acknowledgments

I am most grateful for the helpful friendships of Kenneth Rexroth and his widow Carol Tinker, and for conversations with his daughters Mariana (Mary) and Katherine. I appreciate critiques of an early version of this book by Geoffrey Gardner, editor of *For Rexroth*; by Ben Hansen and poets Antler and Jeff Poniewaz; and especially by James Laughlin, Rexroth's chief publisher and closest literary friend. Also helpful have been Allen Ginsberg, Gary Snyder, Robert Bly, Sam Hamill, and Bradford Morrow, Rexroth's editor and literary executor. I am also grateful to Ihab Hassan for theoretical assistance, and to other former colleagues and students at the University of Wisconsin—Milwaukee, Goddard Collage, Osaka University, and the University of Illinois, where I completed a draft of this book with the help of a visiting associate professorship in the Program in Comparative Literature and the Center for Advanced Study during the Fall of 1982. At Indiana University, 1983–86, the Department of Comparative Literature was good enough to make me a research associate while the book was being completed; and rare publications in the Lilly Library there were useful. Professor Marjorie Perloff at the University of Southern California and Rachelle K. Lerner, writing a doctoral dissertation on Rexroth's cubism at the University of Toronto, exchanged valuable ideas with me about relations between painting and poetry. Brooke Whiting, curator of rare books and literary manuscripts at the University of California at Los Angeles, and William Janko, curator at the University of Southern California, were helpful in my search for documents in their Rexroth collections. My agent, Bonnie R. Crown, and my publisher, James Thorpe III, have been fully supportive.

I also thank, for their helpful understanding of Asian influences, my wife Keiko Matsui Gibson, to whom this book is dedicated, and friends in Japan who collaborated with Rexroth on translations: Professor Sanehide Kodama of Doshisha Women's College in Kyoto, especially for his pioneering studies of Japanese influences on Rexroth; Yuzuru Katagiri of Seika College in Kyoto, the eminent translator of the poetry of Rexroth and other Americans; Yasuyo Morita, Rexroth's secretary in Kyoto; and poets John Solt, former editor of the Asian Studies journal *Stone Lion* at Harvard, Kazuko Shiraishi, and Ikuko Atsumi. These and other friends at Kōya-san, Ehime, Kōchi, Matsuyama, Kwansei Gakuin, Kyushu, and Nihon Universities; Kōbe, Shoin, Hokusei, and Friends' World Colleges; and American Centers arranged lecture tours that allowed me to complete some research in Japan. Zen philosophers Masao Abe, Gishin Tokiwa, and their E A. S. seminars at Myōshinji in Kyoto related Japanese Buddhism to western philosophy in ways that illuminated my study of Rexroth. (Japanese family names follow personal names herein, in the English order, although the order is reversed in Japan.)

I am pleased that Twayne Publishers, G. K. Hall & Company, turned the copyright of my *Kenneth Rexroth*, published in the United States Authors Series in 1972, over to me after the book was sold out. I have included some information from that book in this one, but in a new form and with new interpretations.

Grateful acknowledgment is made to the following for permission to reprint material from the following books:

James Laughlin and New Directions Publishing Corporation for passages from *The Phoenix and the Tortoise*. Copyright 1944 by New Directions Publishing Corporation. Passages from *The New British Poets: an Anthology*. Copyright 1948 by New Directions Publishing Corporation. Passages from *The Signature of All Things*. Copyright 1950 by New Directions Publishing Corporation. Passages from *Beyond the Mountains*. Copyright 1951 by Kenneth Rexroth. Passages from *One Hundred Poems from the Japanese*. Copyright © 1955 by New Directions Publishing Corporation. Passages from *One Hundred Poems from the Chinese*. Copyright © 1956 by New Directions Publishing Corporation. Passages from *Bird in the Bush: Obvious Essays*. Copyright 1947, 1955 by New Directions Publishing

Corporation. Copyright © 1959 by Kenneth Rexroth. Passages from *Assays*. Copyright © 1961 by Kenneth Rexroth. Passages from *An Autobiographical Novel*. Copyright © 1964, 1966 by Kenneth Rexroth. Passages from *The Collected Shorter Poems. Copyright © 1966, 1963, 1962, 1952, 1949, 1940 by Kenneth Rexroth. Copyright © 1956, 1951, 1950, 1944 by New Directions Publishing Corporation. Passages from The Collected Longer Poems.* Copyright 1944, 1950, 1951 by New Directions Publishing Corporation. Copyright © 1968 by New Directions Publishing Corporation. Copyright 1952, 1953 by Kenneth Rexroth. Copyright © 1957, 1967, 1968 by Kenneth Rexroth. Passages from Pierre Reverdy's *Selected Poems*. Copyright © 1955, 1969 by Kenneth Rexroth. Passages from *The Morning Star*. Copyright © 1974, 1976, 1978, 1979 by Kenneth Rexroth. A line from William Carlos Williams's *Collected Later Poems*. Copyright 1944, 1948, 1949, and 1950 by William Carlos Williams. Copyright © by The Estate of William Carlos Williams. Copyright © 1967 by Mrs. William Carlos Williams. Used by permission of James Laughlin for New Directions Publishing Company.

Bradford Morrow for passages from the prefaces to *The Art of Worldly Wisdom*. Copyright © 1953 by Kenneth Rexroth. Passages from *American Poetry in the Twentieth Century*. Copyright © by Herder and Herder, 1971. Passages from *The Elastic Retort*. Copyright © 1973 by Continuum/Seabury Press. Passages from *Excerpts from a Life*. Copyright © 1981 by Kenneth Rexroth and *Conjunctions*. And for passages from Kenneth Rexroth's letters to myself, 1957–1979 (in my possession, to be published as a collection). Used by permission of Bradford Morrow for The Kenneth Rexroth Trust.

Marjorie Perloff, of the University of Southern California, for permission to quote from her letter to me of 11 December 1982.

Father Alberto Huerta, S. J., of the University of San Francisco, for information in his letter to me of 29 July 1985, and permission to reprint a passage from his unpublished eulogy, "*In What Hour*," read at Rexroth's funeral on 11 June 1982.

I am also grateful to editors of my publications on Rexroth listed in the bibliography, and to Mike McDonnell for allowing me to reproduce his portrait of me for the jacket of this volume. The photograph of Rexroth used on the frontispiece is my own work.

Introduction

Kenneth Rexroth lived many lives in the avant-garde of six decades—first in Chicago as a precocious actor, painter, and soapbox poet of revolution after World War I; then on the west coast as Wobbly, cowboy-cook, and mountain-climbing naturalist committed to the protection of the planet long before ecology became a popular concern. Exploring Mexico, New York, Europe, and later Asia, he won international fame as visionary poet, essayist, and translator from half a dozen languages.

He was a contemplative activist, a lyricist of love and nature, a fierce satirist and preacher against injustice, a rowdy comedian and tragic playwright, an erudite culture-critic, a sage of the New Age. A founder of the international objectivist movement and the San Francisco poetry renaissance, he expanded the audience for poetry of high artistic and intellectual caliber. He pioneered in public performances of poetry, often accompanied by live jazz and later by Chinese and Japanese music. Befriending artists, thinkers, workers, feminists, priests, nuns, prostitutes, politicians, musicians, bankers, communists, and fellow anarchists, he wrote from worldly wisdom unique among intellectuals. He collaborated with writers all over the world, assisted many before they became famous, and supported small presses with some of his finest work, while at the same time being published extensively by major publishers. His mother's feminism, in part, motivated his promotion of many women poets, especially those of China and Japan. His lifelong absorption and interpretation of Asian culture advanced the East-West tradition of Whitman, Pound, Yeats, and Waley. Rexroth's poetry of visionary love, at once erotic and spiritual, earthy and transcendent, revealing nirvana in this world, has changed many minds and many lives.

Because much commentary on Rexroth's writings and ideas has appeared in Asia, Europe, and the United States, how is it possible in some surveys of modern poetry for his work to be ignored or only casually mentioned?[1] Just as critics were slow to recognize Whitman, Dickinson, Pound, Williams, Stein, and other innovators, so have many academics been reluctant to take Rexroth seriously; put off, no doubt, by his sweeping attacks on the ivory tower, the New Critics, and the New York literary establishment, as well as upon other vested interests, right and left. His position on the west coast led to the misconception that he was a regional poet; and Asian influences in his work alienated him from some English professors unfamiliar with them. There are those who, finding him more interesting as a personality or thinker than as a writer of poetry, condemn some of it for simplicity or more of it for obscurity. But while emphasizing that poetry is fundamentally vision, Rexroth was as devoted to craftsmanship as were other modern masters. Some of his poetry can be intellectually and stylistically complex, requiring more than a little acquaintance with world literature and thought, but it is no more so than Pound's, Eliot's, or Zukofsky's; and much of his poetry and prose is so direct and personal that he seems to be speaking to us in the same room, or in the mountains overlooking the Pacific.

Perhaps because Rexroth was younger than the classical modernists, not publishing his first book until 1940 when he was thirty-four, and older yet more rebellious than the postwar generation associated with the New Criticism, he has never fit into familiar periods. And though he "discovered" the Beats, he quickly disassociated himself from their movement, as he had withdrawn from objectivism over two decades previously, thus posing special problems for literary historians trying to type him. Incessantly independent and changeable, often alienating friends and allies, he never won the massive following enjoyed by Pound, Eliot, Ginsberg, Olson, Snyder, and others for aesthetic and other reasons. Admirers are sometimes on the defensive about his work, for he could be an outrageous troublemaker, self-righteously ideological, and artistically uneven, but so were lesser writers whose work has received more attention.

Perhaps his anarchic achievement will never find a comfortable home in the academic canon. More important than ranking him is to read his work carefully, interpret it insightfully, and evaluate it philosophically as well as aesthetically. He has been praised for bits and pieces, but rarely for his lifework as a whole. Perhaps he will receive better treatment from critics and professors now that he has been included in *The Norton Anthology of Modern Poetry* and his work is increasingly examined in literary and academic publications.[2]

Rexroth has been hailed by Lawrence Clark Powell as "our greatest man of letters," by Leslie Fiedler as "the last of the great Bohemians," by Hayden Carruth as "our best nature poet," and by George Woodcock as "one of the major poets of our time."[3] In *For Rexroth* he is celebrated by editor Geoffrey Gardner as "the most accomplished and deeply religious poet to write in this country since Whitman," "the American poet who best understands the Japanese culture" by Professor Sanehide Kodama of Kyoto, a "polymathic didact" who is "one of the great love poets of all time" by critic and editor Justus George Lawler, an "anarchic libertarian Wild West magician sage" by poet David Meltzer, and "a great love poet in the most loveless time imaginable" by the late poet James Wright.[4] According to Robert Bly, Rexroth was "the most intelligent literary man in America."[5] Gary Snyder has confirmed his indebtedness to Rexroth; and James Laughlin has said that "Rexroth had a tremendous influence on New Directions and on me . . . Rexroth partly took over the role of Ezra in my life, in that he advised me what to do and put me on to things.[6]

This book is the first to evaluate Rexroth's revolutionary lifework and worldview as a whole, based upon his more than fifty volumes of poems, plays, translations, essays, autobiographies, Japanese and American criticism of his work, our correspondence from 1957 to 1979, and our conversations from 1964 until just before his death on 6 June 1982. Being with him during his tours of Japan, where I taught at Osaka University from 1975 to 1979, was especially helpful.

My thinking has evolved beyond that of my *Kenneth Rexroth*, published in the Twayne United States Authors Series in 1972, which was the first book on Rexroth.[7] Since then two Festschriften and special issues of journals have been devoted to his work, but no other critic has produced a whole book about him excepting Daniela M. Ciani Forza, who covers his work only to 1956 in her Italian study.[8] My 1972 volume, placing him in traditions of "religious anarchism" and "erotic mysticism" (his terms) that include classical, Christian, oriental, and modern prophets, seers, and poets, could not cover the Buddhist poetry of the last decade of his life, his immersion in Japanese culture, some of his best translations and essays, and judgments of his achievement as a whole. In the present volume, which is for the general reader interested in books and ideas as well as for the literary specialist, I have tried to make judgments of his work as objectively as possible while enriching them with insights from our friendship. All I can ask is that readers judge without prejudice the theory and practice of Rexroth's lifework, both for its own sake and for its illumination of Asian, European, and American traditions, reconceived and synthesized.

Not until after Rexroth's death did I realize how his work from beginning to end embodies a contemplative way of interacting with other beings. Rexroth's stormy life was full of anguish from many mistakes—as he mournfully admitted; but his visionary writings suggest how all beings are created, transformed, and united in love, despite massive hatred, violence, and destruction; how we live in universal community, human and cosmic, without usually knowing it; and how human life can be liberated through a revolution in consciousness. This worldview revitalizes and ennobles the human spirit, dangerously threatened by massive military, technological, political, and corporate regimentation that toys with ecological disaster and nuclear annihilation. Denouncing the "social lie" that depersonalizes and destroys, Rexroth offered an alternative way of life, of waking up to the interacting plenitude of creative existence, in a spiritual tradition going back to Shakyamuni, Lao-tzu, Sappho, Jesus, and other heroes of truth, love, and freedom.

I have not tried to write a full biography, but the chapter on his "lives," based on that intellectual adventure story *An Autobiographical Novel*, letters, and other sources, may indicate how Rexroth's personality, art, and thought took various forms as they evolved from contemplative and worldly experiences. "'Poetry Is Vision'—'Vision Is Love'" presents his three poetic modes, symbolism, cubism, and "natural numbers," in a coherent philosophy of literature: poetry is seen as interpersonal communication, originating in contemplation (communion, vision) and recreating community. Chapters 3 and 4 include detailed discussions of his original lyrics, elegies, satires, and revolutionary polemics in *The Collected*

Shorter Poems (herein abbreviated *CSP*, 1966), philosophical reveries in *The Collected Longer Poems* (*CLP*, 1968), Buddhist lyrics in *New Poems* (*NP*, 1974) and *The Morning Star* (*MS*, 1979), and the dramatic tetralogy of the collapse of ancient Greek civilization *Beyond the Mountains* (*BM*, 1951). These volumes and the handy *Selected Poems* (1984), all issued by New Directions, contain virtually all of his published poetry, exclusive of translations. In Chapter 5 his translations are then treated as "acts of sympathy," as he intended them to be. The final chapter on criticism calls for more philosophical interpretations of his work, relating his essays to his theory of literature and to major cultural traditions from which it emerges. The bibliography includes all items about him that I could find in the United States and Japan.

Lives of a Poet: Kenneth Rexroth (1905–1982)

Kenneth Rexroth seems to have passed through several incarnations during his seventy-seven years as poet, translator, essayist, playwright, revolutionary activist, one of America's first abstract painters, and visionary sage.

Born in South Bend, Indiana on 22 December 1905, he lived most of his first twenty-one years in the midwest, primarily in Chicago, where precocious accomplishments brought him fame before he moved to San Francisco in 1927. Making his home there until 1968, when he moved to Montecito in Santa Barbara, he is generally identified as a west coast writer. But extensive study and travel throughout the United States, Europe, and Asia gave his work a cosmopolitanism rare in American poetry; and from 1967 until his death in 1982 his writing and thinking were centered on Japanese Buddhism, though he continued to consider himself a Christian all along.

Did he quixotically charge off in diverse directions at once, or did his various careers express a coherent worldview? How could a poet celebrating love and nature also be committed to social change while at the same time transcending the world as a mystic? Mystics are thought to be ascetically indifferent to falling in love or changing the world, revolutionaries often decry romance as antisocial diversion, and lovers are usually too wrapped up in each other to become fully committed revolutionaries or mystics. Nevertheless, Emma Goldman and Alexander Berkman were revolutionary lovers; Dante and Yeats were erotic mystics; Kropotkin and Tolstoy were saintly anarchists; and like Blake and Whitman, Rexroth was an erotically mystical revolutionary.

He wrote to his second wife:

> This is your own lover, Kenneth, Marie,
> Who someday will be part of the earth
> Beneath your feet; who crowned you once with roses
> Of song; whose voice was no less famous
> Raised against the guilt of his generation.[1]

His voice was righteously raised with comrades like Eli Jacobson, whose bolshevism the anarchist Rexroth opposed but with whom he felt a common commitment:

> We were comrades
> Together, we believed we
> Would see with our own eyes the new
> World where man was no longer
> Wolf to man, but men and women
> Were all brothers and lovers
> Together.[2]

Revolutionary activism, far from distracting him from mysteries of nature, in fact sprang from ecological contemplation that lovingly united inner and outer experience, spirit and body, person and universe:

> The world
> Is alive tonight. I am
> Immersed in living protoplasm,
> That stretches away over
> Continents and seas. I float
> Like a child in the womb.[3]

Here Rexroth alludes to "womb-consciousness," symbolized in the womb-mandala of Tantric Buddhism, a major influence on his worldview because its erotic meditations confirmed his own intuitions of the creative processes of mind, body, and universe, and their fundamental unity. Whereas early Buddhists had viewed sex as a pernicious attachment that caused suffering and delusion, Tantric practices in Nepal and Tibet in the seventh century, and in China and Japan later, involved erotic symbolism and yoga (*yabyum*) as skillful means of realizing universal Being. All of this appealed to Rexroth, whose deepest commitments seemed to flow from a still pool of compassionate wisdom that might be called his Buddha-nature, obscured though it was at times by emotional and intellectual turmoil. He was certainly not a Buddha, for he suffered from attachments, passions, and delusions as much as the rest of us; but he realized in his poetry, more than many poets, how to love in a world of interdependent, interacting beings that mutually reflect each other. This mystical worldview, therefore, embraces eroticism and revolutionary action, both of which may be means of discovering with others the underlying harmony of natural processes. Because he envisioned a community of love in the universe as it is and in human society as it might become, his revolution was anarchistic, aiming at the liberation of consciousness and the perfection of a preexisting community of love, instead of imposing governmental coercion as in communistic, socialistic, and capitalistic states.

Rexroth's autobiographical prose makes clear how visionary, oceanic, nirvanic intimations of eternity, as if he lived in and out of the world simultaneously, generated his vocation as a poet of revolutionary consciousness. He searched through religions, philosophy, and literature for explanations for these experiences, sometimes finding Christian thought appropriate, and later using mostly Buddhist imagery and ideas. For Rexroth, love unites all beings and is never limited to a pair of lovers. His short poems of love and nature and his long philosophical reveries express a sense of the underlying, harmonious interdependence of all things. When he periodically lost this sense of fundamental harmony, he would furiously explode in satire, polemics, and revolutionary prophecy against those people, institutions, and other impersonal forces that threaten love, consciousness, and life itself.

Turning from political action as hopes for humane revolution faded, he developed an organic philosophy, in poetry and prose, that found its fullest expression in Buddhist imagery such as the Net of Indra, in which each jewel in an immense net reflects all others just as each being reflects all others throughout the universe, and each Buddha-world reflects infinite Buddha-worlds. His remarkable achievements in many fields, then, sprang from habitual comtemplation, communion with people he loved and with the cyclical processes of nature, and a sense of community extending from human and earthly realms to galaxies and limitless realms of spirit. If he had lived longer, he might well have produced a philosophical-poetical synthesis of Buddhist and Christian thought with modern ecology, physics, linguistics, and anthropology. That had been his tendency all along.

Before his readings, Rexroth liked to ask whether the audience wanted sex, revolution, or mysticism. Then he would tell about the blond woman who once, from the front row, seductively asked back, "What's the difference?"

An Autobiographical Novel (1966): The Midwest, 1905–1927

The best way to understand the interactions between Rexroth's inner and outer lives, contemplative and worldly experience, mind and action, is to read *An Autobiographical Novel*, covering his first twenty-one years (henceforth abbreviated *AN*). The story was originally dictated into a tape recorder while he was touring Europe with his family, then was transcribed and read on his KPFA radio program in San Francisco, and in 1966 was published by Doubleday. He aimed to understand himself in communion with his daughters and others whom he loved (*AN*, v).

Highly acclaimed in England and America for its portrayal of the poet and his historical milieu, it has been reissued on both sides of the Atlantic.[4] Like Yeats's *Autobiographies* and Wordsworth's *Prelude* the book reveals "the growth of the poet's mind," but Rexroth seems to have been more worldly than either of the earlier poets. His feet were on the ground, and on the pavements of Chicago during the Roaring Twenties. Deadpan objectivity, photographic description, witty anecdotes, adventurous story-telling, and incessant intellectual inquiry sweep us into his stormy life. Regardless of inaccuracies that biographers are sure to turn up, Rexroth's life-story shows how his creative powers as painter and poet emerged from his contemplation of the universe, how his ideas developed through personal encounters, vast reading, the practice of translation, and an incessant spiritual quest. Like Augustine and Rousseau, Rexroth told his life as a search for ultimate values, though his differed radically from theirs. Rexroth's sense of life came closest to that of Tu Fu, his favorite nondramatic poet, who seemed to be saying in his work that "only men's steadfastness, love, magnanimity, calm, and compassion redeem the nightbound world" (*AN*, 319).

These values inhere in the contemplative, visionary experiences discussed at length. When he was four or five years old, observing a wagon-load of new-mown hay, he claims that "An awareness, not a feeling, of timeless, spaceless, total bliss occupied me or I occupied it completely" (*AN*, 338). The careful wording shows that bliss was not merely his feeling, but something that he was aware of beyond time and space, a "normal and natural life" transcending the tribulations of ordinary life and yet immanent in physical existence. So he seems to have had intuitions of nirvana or heaven on earth. When he was eleven and his mother died, "a great sense of peace and well-being came over me as though I, too, had gone to a heaven which was all one calm, limitless, vision" (*AN*, 77). When he had a high fever from flu, he terrified his father by saying, "The whole room is filled with silver lines like thousands of spider webs of light. They all come together over there where there is a spot so bright you can't stand to look at it. That is the other me on the other side of the universe" (*AN*, 91).

At fifteen, he plunged into philosophy for explanations of such visionary experiences of "communion" (*AN*, 152)—a term that implies Christian love, but he goes on to show how other religions and philosophies also contributed to his worldview. So speculation characterizes much of his work, especially the longer poems, though he realized that it could not finally explain visionary life or express the love and wisdom flowing from it. Instead, in order to transmit his deepest experiences in poetry, he came to rely upon such powerful images from Tantric Buddhism as sexual bliss with female deities, symbolizing the union of compassion and transcendental wisdom, and sun and moon as symbols of enlightenment.

As a youth in retreat at Holy Cross Monastery near Poughkeepsie, N. Y., he considered becoming an Anglo-Catholic monk; but though he experienced rapture throughout Holy Week, he did not feel "called" to this vocation (*AN*, 334–35). Instead, he sought enlightenment in erotic mysticism and sacramental marriage, enthused by the writings of D. H. Lawrence, H. G. Wells, and many ancient mystics. He described marital bliss with his first wife, Andrée Dutcher, an anarchist painter who suffered from epilepsy and kleptomania, as "total identification" (*AN*, 358). Similar experiences generated "When We with Sappho" and other ecstatic love poems. This poem, beginning with Rexroth's version of Sappho's apple-blossom poem, shows how he and his beloved transcend historical fact, for she is "Not like a body, not like a separate thing / But like a nimbus that hovers / Over every other thing in all the world." The intensity of direct address mounts from the hypnotic repetition of "summer" to the startling imperatives of "Lean back. Give me your mouth." The lovers' bliss illuminates the world, ancient as well as present, human and natural: "I will press / Your summer honeyed flesh into the hot / Soil, into the crushed, acrid herbage / Of midsummer." Afterwards they rest and savor Sappho's poem. Finally in silence their bodies slip away like the sun as they move toward death with Sappho.[5]

Love is, then, the dominant emotion of Rexroth's poetry and prose: love of women, of community, of nature, of poetry and the other arts, of innumerable Buddha-worlds (dimensions of universal mind). Love is at once erotic and transcendent, flowing through him and the universe, reflecting all beings in every being, transforming life into poetry, uniting individuals in communities. His satirical and polemical poems attack those who deny, block, or pervert love into destructive power. His elegies commemorate his loves in recognition of inevitable cycles of creation through destruction. His translations came about through sympathetic identification with poets of many cultures. So all of his poetry and poetics, his philosophizing and acting in the world to savor and improve it, flow fundamentally from love.

In his tales of family, friends, lovers, and spiritual and literary masters, we learn how he enacted roles of rebel, prophet, and bard from ancient times as well as from the American tradition of conscientious dissent and revolt, encouraged by his parents' noblesse oblige. The family's values were those of the American struggle in defense of natural rights of conscience as proclaimed in the revolution for national independence, in Jeffersonian and Jacksonian democracy, frontier populism, New England transcendentalism and abolitionism, the spiritual and political radicalism of European immigrants, Debsian socialism, the Industrial Workers of the World, feminism, and other movements for social reform in opposition to militarism, bureaucratic repression, ecclesiastical authoritarianism, political persecution, and capitalistic profit making at the expense of "life, liberty, and the pursuit of happiness."

Like Whitman and Williams, and unlike Pound and Eliot, he

never abandoned American experience, even as he absorbed European and Asian cultures, for he felt no fundamental contradiction between his labors as a Wobbly logger and his delight in translating Greek and Chinese poetry. He took himself for granted, accepting the universality of his own experience instead of submitting to external authorities for discipline. So mystical realizations are presented as matter-of-factly as political struggles.

The earliest Rexroths were thirteenth century Harz mountain peasants and scholars and West German officials, some perhaps Jewish. In America, the first Rexroths were pietists and radicals, marrying with Indians, Blacks, and Irishmen, and settling mostly in Ohio. Kenneth's father was Charles Rexroth, an unsuccessful but high-living pharmacist of considerable sophistication, wit, and charm, a drinking companion of Theodore Dreiser, James Whitcomb Riley, Eugene Fields, George Ade and other famous midwestern writers; and his mother was Delia (or Della) Reed, a woman of aesthetic sensibility who had dropped out of Oberlin College for a brief business career with a suffragette before her marriage.

Less than a year after Kenneth was born, the family moved to Elkhart, Indiana, where his mother began educating him with methods similar to the Montessori system, an Indian soon taught him nature lore, and his father later equipped him with a scientific laboratory. Kenneth's childhood seems to have been idyllic until, in his fifth year or so, his father had the first of a series of financial crises, a couple of years later his mother's lung hemorrhaged, and his father began drinking so heavily that Kenneth was emotionally distanced from him and thereafter despised drunks. Despite these tribulations, the family visited England and Europe later that year and traveled as far as Constantinople, initiating Kenneth as a world-traveler. They then settled in Battle Creek, Michigan, for about three years, but occasionally visited New York, where he met such famous Bohemians as James Gibbon Huneker, Sadakichi Hartman, and the anarchist lovers Alexander Berkman and Emma Goldman. Meanwhile, as his parents had love affairs, little Kenneth began to have his own in a dream-world inspired by the utopian Oz books. When he was ten, his parents moved with him briefly to Chicago, then separated, reunited, and returned to Elkhart, where his mother died in 1916 of gangrene of the lung. Devoted to her as an ideal mother and liberated woman, he commemorated her in several elegies, calling her "a fierce lover, / A wild wife, an animal / Mother."[6] For a couple of years he then lived in Toledo, Ohio, with his paternal grandmother and then with his father, who died in 1918 (*AN*, 91). If Kenneth had learned to debate ideas from his father, he had learned to love deeply from his mother; so in his poems, thinking rises from love and, finding no ultimate answers, sinks back into love.

The boy then lived in Chicago off and on until 1927, first with his mother's sister, then alone in his own studio. Residing in James T. Farrell's neighborhood, he later appeared as a fat boy named Kenny in *Studs Lonigan*.[7] He attended classes at the Art Institute, Edmund Burke Grammar School, and eventually Englewood High School, but his real education was extracurricular, as he began to associate with many celebrities and become known as poet, theater director and actor, abstract painter, journalist, and political activist. Observing Communists and reading Lenin, he rejected bolshevism because of its militarism and centralized authoritarianism and for the rest of his life remained an anarchist, opposed to centralized government and all other collectivities. A poem called "The Bad Old Days" tells how, after reading Upton Sinclair's *The Jungle* and H. G. Wells's *The Research Magnificent*, and seeing for himself, in the stockyards area of Chicago, "Debauched and exhausted faces, / Starved and looted brains,"[8] he took a revolutionary vow that is probably the one of Eugene Debs in *The Dragon and the Unicorn*: "While there is a lower class, / I am in it. While there is / A criminal element, / I am of it. Where there is / A soul in jail, I am not free."[9] Paradoxically, he also believed that he "belonged to a special elite whose mission it was to change the world" and that his primary way of doing this was through poetry (*AN*, 149).

During his fifteenth year, the most intellectually active time of his life, he began translating poetry, Sappho's "Apple Orchard" first of all, then other poems from the Greek, Chinese, and Japanese, depending on Judith Gautier's French versions of oriental poems until he could read the originals. He visited classes at the University of Chicago, but never pursued a degree. He claimed to have begun his first long philosophical poem, *The Homestead Called Damascus*, as early as 1920, and to have finished it in 1925, during his first major love affair, with a social worker ten years older than himself named Shirley Johnson ("Leslie Smith" in his poetry), and a minor fling with a Jewish student named Ruth at the University of Chicago. The poem's symbolist style and Christian questing for spiritual renewal were strongly affected by his discovery of *The Waste Land* in the *Dial* of 1922, which he imagined to be revolutionary until realizing its reactionary thrust. Because of his reaction to symbolism generally and Eliot's work in particular, he did not publish the poem as a whole for thirty-two years (*AN*, 191–201, 255–58).

Accompanying Shirley to Smith College, he met the imprisoned Sacco and Vanzetti, whose anarchist saintliness permanently deepened his radical commitments. In New York he tried sexual yoga with a free-thinking disciple of Mahatma Gandhi. Back in Chicago he acted in plays by Pirandello and other modernists and joyfully discovered Middle English and Latin poetry, philosophy, and theology, which attracted him to the sacramental system of Catholicism, especially its Anglican expression, though he remained heterodox in thought and behavior. Hitchhiking to Seattle in 1924, he worked as a logger and participated in the Industrial Workers of the World, then explored primitive life in the Ozarks before settling again in Chicago, where he led a dada movement and studied anthropology on his own, inspired by Edward Sapir, who seems to have understood Rexroth's poetics of communion and communication.[10]

Breaking up with Shirley, he explored the southwest and Mexico, meeting the D. H. Lawrence circle, which hardly resembled the community of love that he had been seeking, then worked with both cowboys and Indians on the west coast. He studied Wittgenstein, but rejected the *Tractatus* for Duns Scotus's ontology, eventually finding that no philosophy offered final answers or embodied the wisdom that he craved. Working his way on a ship to Europe, he met Aragon, Soupault, Tzara, Cendrars, and other literary heroes in Paris, but returned to the American west after Alexander Berkman advised him not to become another expatriate. He was soon mountain-climbing and training horses in Montana, then met Rivera, Orozco, and other revolutionary artists in Mexico.

In 1927 he and his bride Andrée hitchhiked from Chicago to California, where he was to make his home thereafter, arriving just before news of Sacco and Vanzetti's executions in Boston shattered revolutionary hopes—an event commemorated in some of his finest elegies.[11] In the same year he completed "Prolegomena to a Theodicy," his second long philosophical revery, a Christian vision of hell and heaven in the cubist mode, begun in 1925 but not published until 1932.

The first twenty-one years of Rexroth's life must have been even more complex than could be indicated in the concentrated, rapidly paced narrative of *An Autobiographical Novel*. It seems that he was never idle nor at a loss for discovery and creation. And during his years of being based in Chicago, especially the last seven, his religious, mystical, philosophical, political, erotic, and artistic perspectives coalesced in a way that determined the rest of his lifework.

Excerpts from a Life (1981): California, 1927–1948

Although by the age of twenty-one Rexroth had had more intellectual adventures than most people have in a lifetime, the move to California in 1927 initiated an even greater leap forward. In this second phase of his development, centered in San Francisco until 1968, his poetry, drama, translations, culture criticism, revolutionary activism, and painting reached fruition, with most of his major writings being published before his attention centered on Asia as never before.

From an additional installment of Rexroth's autobiography, *Excerpts from a Life*, published in 1981 and covering the years 1927–1948, we learn how the Rexroths settled in San Francisco, how they turned from geometric painting to a rendering of organic forms as they climbed mountains, observed landscapes, and made friends with the photographer Edward Weston, the painter Hilaire Hiler, the poet-critic Yvor Winters, the lesbian-anarchist poet Elsa Gidlow, and a young Russian genius, Mark Kliorin, who eventually disappeared in Moscow.

In 1929 Rexroth began publishing in magazines, and in 1932 made his first major international breakthrough as a leading cubist in the Revolution of the Word. Two versions of "Prolegomena to a Theodicy" appeared in *An "Objectivists" Anthology* in Le Beausset, Var, France, in 1932: the poet's original and a revision by editor Louis Zukofsky that Rexroth repudiated in the same issue.[12]

Rexroth's comprehension of Marxism, especially the theory of capitalistic self-alienation at the center of Marx's humanist philosophy, matured in response to the Great Depression and international crises; so during a visit to New York he joined the first John Reed Club because of its broad representation of diverse viewpoints at that time, despite his objections to bolshevism, which he thought had perverted Marx's ideas. Andrée, on the other hand, joined the Communist Party, went insane, and attempted suicide. They separated, Rexroth fell in love with Marie Cass, a nurse, and married her in 1940, after Andrée had died in an epileptic seizure.

The same year, *In What Hour*, consisting of thirty-one poems of revolution, love, and nature, was published by Macmillan and the next year won a California Silver Medal Award. This brilliant first book, the product of twenty years of writing and more than a decade of publishing in periodicals and anthologies in Europe and the United States, includes cubist poems as well as poems in natural speech. Though critics admired the nature poems and Rexroth's intellect and artistry, they had difficulty grasping the serious quest of the poet, through the poems of revolutionary hope, struggle, defeat, and despair, towards an organic philosophy in which value is naturally emergent in geological and biological, social and artistic, processes.[13] The quest zigzags like a mountain trail, so dark at times that it is apparently impassable before suddenly brightening. As Rexroth confronted social, economic, and military crises of the 1930s from mountains under stars, he realized in these poems how creation emerges from destruction, universally.

Rexroth saw World War II as a supreme symptom of an exploitative, authoritarian, dehumanizing, and disintegrating "civilization," rather than simply a conflict between democracy and fascism. Nor did he support the Soviet state, which in his opinion had betrayed humane ideals of social revolution. Like Kenneth Patchen, Paul Goodman, William Everson, William Stafford, and other pacifist and anarchist writers, he refused on ethical grounds to kill impersonal "enemies," even for a government less unjust than the totalitarian states. Instead of joining a war effort that he believed would perpetuate injustices, he did what he could to advance the values of love, cooperation, and community. He was, therefore, constantly and often dangerously threatened by those uncritically supporting the war, including former friends from the Left; and his position was unique even among pacifists, who were generally from traditional peace churches. As a conscientious objector, he worked as an orderly in a psychiatric hospital, where he was permanently injured by a violent patient. He also gave humanitarian aid to Japanese-Americans, threatened by evacuation and incarceration, who in turn helped him explore oriental culture.

The study and practice of Buddhist and Christian contemplation show up in his second book, *The Phoenix and the Tortoise*, published in 1944 by New Directions. According to the preface, the poems were written after 1940, but at least one exception must be the translation of Sappho's apple-blossom poem, which he had written as a youth. In a style of classical clarity the poet moves from desperation, abandon, and resignation in response to cultural collapse, shown in the Hellenistic, Byzantine, and Roman paraphrases, through "erotic mysticism" (in the original poems of love and nature) into a consciousness of "universal responsibility" through "sacramental marriage," which generated the long title poem in response to World War II. The poems were reprinted: the title poem in *The Collected Longer Poems*; the thirty-seven short ones and a few of the twenty-six translations in *The Collected Shorter Poems*; and most of the translations and imitations from Chinese, Greek, and Latin in various collections of translations. The book was enthusiastically reviewed and won him another California Silver Medal Award the following year.[14]

After the war, in a worldwide upsurge of apocalyptic hopes for a new way of life despite cold war militarism, Rexroth helped organize the Libertarian League for a thorough study of revolutionary thought and action from an anarchist perspective. He also organized weekly poetry readings that spawned the San Francisco renaissance years before the Beats appeared, and which led to the establishment of the Poetry Center at the San Francisco State College (now University).[15] Distinguishing his own ethics, based on a personal-mystical sense of universal community, from statist politics (Republican, Democratic, communist, socialist, fascist) on the one hand and the mindless amorality of many Beats and hippies on the other, Rexroth claimed that his literary and political activities had helped spread a new style of cultural revolt across the continent and abroad (*Excerpts*, 61). Rejecting the "social lie" that coerces people into serving dehumanizing institutions, Rexroth uncompromisingly advocated being true to love, friendship, knowledge, relentless inquiry, critical thought, and the creative spirit of nature and art.

Organic Christian Personalism: California and Europe, 1947–1967

In 1947, Viking published Rexroth's edition of *Selected Poems of D. H. Lawrence*, containing his vigorous introduction to the erotic-visionary-prophetic poetry, an important influence on his own. Though Rexroth had been publishing criticism for almost two decades in periodicals, the Lawrence essay, written as imaginatively as his poetry, brought him international fame as an important critic at odds with the impersonal formalism of the New Critics and other academics.

He was divorced from Marie the next year, married Marthe Larsen, and traveled to Europe on a Guggenheim Fellowship. It was renewed in 1949, when, in his anthology, *The New British Poets*, his long essay on the neo-romanticism of Dylan Thomas, Denise Levertov, George Barker, Hugh MacDiarmid, and others who were expanding the emotional and intellectual range of poetry across the Atlantic effectively introduced their work to many American readers.

Also in 1949, *The Art of Worldly Wisdom*, a collection of his cubist poems written between 1920 and 1932, was published in an effort to revive the Revolution of the Word. This third volume of Rexroth's poetry included his second long poem, retitled "A Prolegomenon to a Theodicy," shorter poems, and the first of many manifesto-like introductions to his books. But because of improper printing after the director of the Decker Press in Prairie City, Illinois, was murdered, the collection was reissued, as Rexroth had originally intended it, in 1953 by the Golden Goose Press in Sausalito. The first edition was dedicated to his late wife Andrée, and the second to the anarchist poet and painter Kenneth Patchen, to whom Rexroth then felt closer than to any other American writer, for Patchen was extending techniques abandoned after this book. In the 1953 preface, Rexroth belligerently proclaims:

> I write for one and only one purpose, to overcome the invincible ignorance of the traduced heart. My poems are acts of force and violence directed against the evil which murders us all. If you like, they are designed not just to overthrow the present State, economic system, and Church, but all prevailing systems of human collectivity altogether . . . I wish to speak to and for all those who have

had enough of the Social Lie, the Economics of Mass Murder, the Sexual Hoax, and the Domestication of Conspicuous Consumption.

Such polemics turned off some readers, for the time was not ripe for revolution of any kind.[16] During the McCarthyite years of the Korean War, Rexroth was one of the few writers to proclaim publicly an uncompromising faith in human liberation from all forms of coercion, winning him admiration from some, but contempt from many, including Stalinists who resented his attacks on the Soviet Union. Not all of the poems in *The Art of Worldly Wisdom*, however, were radical in style or subject. The best poems in the collection, in fact, the sequence for Leslie Smith, his Chicago lover, are tender love lyrics of much wider appeal than the cubist and rhetorical pieces (*CSP*, 31–36).

From this quiet side of Rexroth's sensibility came *The Signature of All Things* (1950), the fourth book of his own poetry, including some of his most enduring personal lyrics and translations of mystical love and nature and a preface affirming that "the integral person is more revolutionary than any program, party, or social conflict." The book's title is borrowed from Jacob Boehme, the seventeenth century Christian mystic who, along with Buber, Schweitzer, Suzuki, and Kropotkin, influenced the spiritual anarchism of Rexroth's poems. Their style, he says, is influenced less by contemporary poetry than by folksongs from around the world, primitive and ancient songs, and "directly communicative poetry" by Burns, Landor, Blake, Christina Rosetti, Tennyson, and others. The syllabic prosody that had become familiar in Rexroth's non-cubist work is concisely explained. Though the book is dedicated to Marie, to whom the most erotic poems are addressed, Marthe, his third wife, bore their first daughter, Mary, the year that the volume was published.[17]

Rexroth's poetic, philosophical, and visionary powers are epitomized in *Beyond the Mountains*, four verse tragedies on the disintegration of the Greek world, and of civilization in general, influenced by Japanese No drama as well as by Sophocles and Euripides. They were published separately in periodicals, then altogether as a book in 1951. *Phaedra* was premiered in St. Louis in June, 1951, directed by James Walsh, who acted also in the New York premiere by the Living

Theatre of the tetralogy as a whole—including also *Iphigenia at Aulis*, *Hermaios*, and *Berenike*—directed by Julian Beck and starring Judith Malina, 30 December 1951–20 January 1952.[18] The plays' theme of spiritual commitment in the face of collapsing civilization was amplified the next year in *The Dragon and the Unicorn*, Rexroth's fifth book of nondramatic poetry and his fourth long philosophical poem, evolving from his travels in postwar Europe, under the threat of World War III. The poem amplifies the erotic, organic personalism, still predominantly Christian but with vivid Buddhist themes and imagery, of *The Phoenix and the Tortoise*, the poem which it most closely resembles; but Rexroth's style has become much stronger and more flexible in this longest of his poems.[19]

In 1952 Rexroth's first full collection of translations, *Fourteen Poems by O. V. de L. Milosz*, most of them done years before from the French, confirmed his already recognized accomplishments as a translator. A year after a second daughter was born in 1954, his children were honored in the whimsical *A Bestiary for My Daughters Mary and Katherine*. Also in 1955, *One Hundred Poems from the French* and the ever-popular *One Hundred Poems from the Japanese* established him as a major translator who was extending Pound's attempt to bridge Asian and occidental cultures. *Thou Shalt Not Kill: A Memorial for Dylan Thomas*, his most powerful and renowned protest poem against the worldwide culture of violence, ripped through the reactionary decade. This blistering poem and the *Bestiary* were reprinted with other poems of protest, satire, and affection in his sixth full book of original poetry, *In Defense of the Earth* in 1956, dedicated to his daughters. A short preface reaffirms the visionary and prophetic role of poetry in opposition to a destructive society.[20]

Also in 1956 *Thirty Spanish Poems of Love and Exile* and *One Hundred Poems from the Chinese* increased his popularity as a translator.[21] He taught at San Francisco State College, though having never completed high school, he bristled at academic restrictions. And in 1957 he received a Chapelbrook Award and the Eunice Tietjens Award from *Poetry* magazine.

Meanwhile his fame was dramatically spreading because of worldwide attention to the San Francisco renaissance and the Beat Generation after he had introduced Allen Ginsberg and other poets at a reading at the Six Gallery in San Francisco in 1955. More than any other American poet, he had kept alive, through dark years of war and cold war, the spirit of revolt, protest, and liberation, even when it was widely believed that conformity and conservatism were permanent. His support of the Beat movement was critical and temporary, for he objected to the ignorance, amorality, and commercialism of some of its participants, but he long praised Ginsberg as a major poet of visionary protest and remained close friends with Ferlinghetti, McClure, and especially Snyder, whose work has the closest affinities with his own.[22]

In 1957 *The Homestead Called Damascus*, his first long philosophical poem, the symbolist reverie of two brothers' quest, completed in 1926, was first published in *The Quarterly Review of Literature* with Lawrence Lipton's introductory essay, and won a Longview Award.[23] He also received a Eunice Tietjens Award from *Poetry* magazine, a $1000 Shelley Memorial Award from the Poetry Society of America, a Chapelbrook Award, and an Amy Lowell Fellowship.

Bird in the Bush: Obvious Essays, Rexroth's first whole book of criticism, issued in 1959, and *Assays* in 1961, extended the already powerful influence of his erudite prose that had been appearing in periodicals in support of the new American poetry, and projecting a bolder, more imaginative comprehension of world culture than was evident among most academics.[24]. Also in 1961, he and Marthe were divorced. The next year, *Poems from the Greek Anthology* reminded readers that his poetic practice and theory were grounded in western classics as well as in those from Asia.

In 1963, *The Homestead Called Damascus* was republished as a booklet with a foreword by James Laughlin,[25] along with *Natural Numbers: New and Selected Poems*, a small, quiet assortment from his previous books, with a few new poems for his daughters.[26] He was also writing a column for the *San Francisco Examiner* and teaching a course in art history and appreciation at the San Francisco Art Institute. The next year he received a grant from The National Academy of Arts and Letters, taught at San Francisco State College, and in the summer was poet-in-residence at the University of Wisconsin—Milwaukee. In 1965 he won a William Carlos Williams Award from *Contact* magazine.

As youth rebellion boiled against racial discrimination, academic restrictions, and especially the war in Southeast Asia, Rexroth spoke out clearly and forcefully against injustices, but published no new protest poems after 1963. Why? Perhaps rebellion could not defeat the "social lie," against which he had said all that he could say, or so he thought. Moreover, he had come to the tragic conclusion that those who rule the world would destroy it through ecological catastrophe or nuclear war. They

> are pushing all this pretty
> Planet, Venice, and Palladio,
> And you and me, and the golden
> Sun, nearer and nearer to
> Total death. Nothing can stop them.[27]

In 1966 *An Autobiographical Novel* and *The Collected Shorter Poems*, containing new work and poetry from nine previously published books, climaxed his career so far.[28]

The Buddha's Way: Asia, 1967–1982

Rexroth made enduring poetic, philosophical, ecological, and utopian contributions to the holistic worldview evolving in the counterculture, while condemning drugs, mindless music, senseless activism, and other stupid excesses along with the alienation, bigotry, coercion, and warfare of the established culture. Throughout his life he had been developing an organic philosophy of mind and community long before most intellectuals had recognized the ecological basis of human life and thought.

Believing that the disintegration of western civilization was being hastened by the so-called technological revolution, he turned increasingly to traditional Asian culture, which had influenced him from the beginning of his career, but which had remained subordinated to Christian themes until 1967, when it predominated over western thought in his work. In that year, after visiting Japan and other Asian countries for the first time, and Europe again, on a world tour made possible by a grant from the Rockefeller Foundation and an *Akademische Austausdienst* Award from West Berlin, he wrote at Daitokuji Zen Temple in Kyoto *The Heart's Garden, The Garden's Heart.* It was his fifth long poem, a Buddhist reverie in his most sensuously melodic style, rich in allusions to Japanese literature, in which he seems to attain satori. This masterpiece of living in the Tao, dedicated to his daughters and to Carol Tinker, was published first as

a book in 1967, with graphic designs by the poet, and the next year in
The Collected Longer Poems.[29]

The long poems, read consecutively with the aid of the preface
to the collection, display the development of Rexroth's worldview
from the resignation of *Homestead* to the apocalyptic *Prolegomenon,*
then through the erotic-organic personalism of *The Phoenix and the
Tortoise* and *The Dragon and the Unicorn,* to the realization of dharma
in Japan.[30] Buddhist influences had appeared in *Homestead,* and after
a twenty-year hiatus had thematically and imagistically shaped *The
Phoenix and the Tortoise,* which nevertheless was centrally Christian,
but they had intensified until by 1967 his outlook was predominantly
Buddhist.[31]

Like his friend Thomas Merton, Rexroth had seen no fundamental contradiction between Christian and Buddhist contemplative experience, in the "peace that passeth understanding" beyond
words and ideas. As a youth he had understood Buddhism as a "pure
religious empiricism . . . the Noble Eight Fold Path, whose culmination is the 'unruffledness'—Nirvana—which underlies reality."[32]

He had anarchistically explored the Eight Fold Path of morality
(right speech, conduct, and livelihood), meditation (right effort,
mindfulness, and contemplation), and wisdom (right views and
aspirations). His morality was not monastic but revolutionary, based
on responsibility for all humanity, like that of a bodhisattva who
renounces nirvana until all beings enter it. He practiced yoga off and
on, but did not believe "in sitting zazen, facing the wall and strain-
ing, as at stool, for satori. Satori is an invisible mist, which envelops
you unaware and finally never goes away."[33]

In 1968 *Classics Revisited,* his most popular collection of essays
from *Saturday Review,* vastly expanded his fame as a critic. Having
lived in San Francisco for forty-one years, Rexroth became so dis-
gusted with the increase of drugs and crime there that he moved to
Santa Barbara in the fall to begin teaching on the University of
California campus there.[34]

In 1969 he vigorously defended cubism in the introduction to
Pierre Reverdy Selected Poems and in translations therein; and the year
after that he swung from west to east again in *Love in the Turning Year:
One Hundred More Poems from the Chinese.* Also in 1970 *The Alternative Society: Essays from the Other World* centered on American
literature and soicety in the face of nuclear extinction; and *With Eye*

and Ear related eastern and western literature and religion. He was so firmly established in American intellectual life, despite his relentless objections to it, that in the spring of that year, just before campuses exploded all over the country in massive strikes against the war in Southeast Asia, he was offered a professorship at the University of Wisconsin—Milwaukee which he declined because students at the University of California at Santa Barbara were demanding that he continue teaching there.

Because Rexroth's spiritual life, like Merton's, was never an escape from humanity, he had become increasingly concerned about the buildup of the war in Southeast Asia and political repression of opponents to it. Though he persistently spoke out against the war and other injustices, generally sympathized with the Movement, and admired the honest commitment of many activists, he did not conceal his contempt for participants who were stupid, amoral, or totalitarian. Some of them, in turn, distrusted his anarchism, considered him above the battle, did not know his earlier protest poems, did not care for his music and poetry performances, or saw no "relevance" in the Buddhist poems that he was writing at this time. He grew increasingly dubious about confrontational opposition as the war worsened. Ever since the execution of Sacco and Vanzetti he had seen idealistic rebellions crushed. He knew that even the most militant demonstrations would not bring down the military-industrial complex and usher in utopia.[35] He wrote me on 3 June 1970:

> As the world economic crisis II shuts down radical melodrama, massive confrontation, calls for "general strikes" observed only by tiny minorities, all this will have to change to infiltration, organization, long term planning. The past decade of adventurism was purely a function of the affluent society. Jerry Rubin is Hugh Hefner in dirty whiskers. Eventually of course we will have new armies of unemployed, dispossessed and starving. But now is the time for the cadres to consolidate and hang on to any strategic positions they've gained. *Nobody* knows now how to plan, organize, train—or what for. *So don't quit!*
>
> I think the "crisis program" here was a fine idea. A "hard strike" would not have been pulled off. There'd have been a mass picket line for a couple of days, arrests, club-

bings, gas, shootings, and then it would have been over. As it is students are getting credit for "crisis classes" in the theory and practice of social conflict, the economics of the war economy, the history of revolution, *etc etc* and more credit for canvassing door to door in Santa Barbara, and union to union, and lunch hour factory to factory, and store to store.

> Rubin was just here—He screamed "Kill your parents! Kill your parents! Kill your parents!" and the whole stadium booed. By the time he was through over half of his audience had walked out, leaving elderly teenyboppers screaming as they used to for Benny Goodman.

Rexroth's political critiques might seem to have nothing to do with Buddhism, but in fact the war and resistance to it heightened awareness of the universal suffering of humanity, which the Buddha claimed resulted from attachments. The disillusioning process of history, so familiar to Rexroth, had deepened his interest in the Buddha's way of liberation, as opposed to purely political methods. When I asked him whether certain meditation experiences might be satori, he explained to me in his letter of 23 September 1970 the difference between Buddhist and Christian realization:

> My. My. First time? I've always thought that's what part of the mind is always doing anyway—you just get a sharp focusing of attention on that level and a kind of hypertrophy of importance. It's the opposite of the mystical experience where there is a gradual dying out of any "importance" into IMPORTANCE and a sense of peace and contentless where you occupy CONTENT—the "meaning of meaning." What a disappointment that title [of I. A. Richard's book] was in the 20's when we expected something quite different. Of course in completion all polarities and antitheses merge. Love to all   Kenneth

As the Movement collapsed, Rexroth tried to keep alive radical ideas in his writing of *Communalism*. In 1971 he reported, "This has been a year of retreat. Everybody is scared after the 69–70 pogroms against students & blacks. Reagan's bloodbath policy has worked so far." Unlike Gary Snyder and others, he saw little hope of the

Movement's securing itself in communes: "Most of the country ones sound like Wheeler's ranch, shit on the ground, crash pads of an unrelieved nightmare of drugs & disorder—essentially a phenomenon of breakdown not revolution—and totally upper middleclass." (Undated letter to me.)

In 1971, his longest literary study, *American Poetry in the Twentieth Century*, showed how writing had emerged from complex regional, ethnic, intellectual, and artistic communities; and more quiet nature poetry from his Japanese experience, *Sky Sea Birds Trees Earth House Beasts Flowers*, was dedicated to Carol Tinker and Gary Snyder.

In 1972, after he had commented on a draft of my *Kenneth Rexroth*, it was corrected and published.[36] He returned to Japan for a Japanology conference in Tokyo, and *The Orchid Boat: Women Poets of China*, translations done with Ling Chung, contributed to the rising consciousness of women in literature. In 1973 *The Elastic Retort: Essays in Literature and Ideas* offered more "Classics Revisited" and other pieces on Japanese and western religion and culture.

In 1974, after marrying the poet Carol Tinker in an Episcopal service in Santa Barbara, he lived with her in a Kyoto farmhouse with eight hundred year old beams, a tea ceremony room, and rare calligraphies. For about a year he gave readings and lectures throughout Japan and other Asian countries, explored cultural traditions, and worked on new poetry and prose. *One Hundred More Poems from the Japanese*[37] and *New Poems* (a short collection of work in progress)[38] appeared in 1974, along with his essay on the art of literature in the fifteenth edition of *The Encyclopaedia Brittanica*, followed the next year by the fullest exposition of his social philosophy, *Communalism, from the Neolithic to 1900*, his longest historical study.

Our correspondence on Buddhism indicates his disappointment in finding many Japanese less sophisticated than he had expected.

That's quite a letter! I have quoted it to Japanese & Indian (I just was at an "East-West" discussion in Bombay) intellectuals and it amazes them—to whom Buddhism, Hinduism, much less Tantrism is anathema, and represents only the blackest reaction and commercialism. In Japan,

some of the youngest, influenced by Snyder, have taken up
their own, or Gary's "Buddhism," which is as much a
recent construct as Suzuki (or Buber's "Zen Judaism") and
a kind of Neo-Tantrism is popular among a very few
intellectuals in India, mostly artists. Most Japanese are
totally ignorant of the very existence of philosophical Buddhism or have ever read the Lotus, or ever heard of the
Lankavatara or the Avatamsaka—or know the difference
between a Buddha & a Bodhisattva." [1 February 1975]

Buddhism is for burials, Shinto for weddings—both
thoroly [sic] commercial & as bankrupting as bar mitzvahs.
[1 June 1975]

A Japanese would as likely to seek philosophy from a
Buddhist monk as you would from a "mortician." [3 July
1975]

He denounced Zen as a religion of militarists, millionaires, and
hippies, but excepted Daisetz Suzuki, whom he had met as a boy in
Michigan, and whom he admired as a creative thinker. Similarly,
though he loathed the sentimentality of many haiku, the poetic
offspring of Zen, he admired the great accomplishments of Bashō
and Shiki.

Despite his complaints he loved many Japanese friends, authors
ancient and modern, temples, shrines, and gardens, about which he
spoke enthusiastically when we met in Kyoto just before his and
Carol's return to Santa Barbara. Back in America he denounced it:

After Japan the culture shock is too much. This is the
greatest military despotism since Assyria, governed by
fools & feared and hated by every nation on earth . . . I don't
want to be part of the collective guilt. I do not have a male
friend in Santa Barbara who is not a foreigner! I don't know
what American men are talking about and I have nothing to
say to them . . . I wish I was 35 years younger. I
would . . . change my citizenship. [1 February 1976]

Deepening Japanese influences had shaped the poignant lyrics in
The Silver Swan and *On Flower Wreath Hill*, the Buddhist sequence of
eight short poems written in a Kyoto cemetery as he had anticipated

death, published in 1976 and dedicated to Yasuyo Morita, Rexroth's secretary in Kyoto who contributed calligraphies on the cover and title page, while he had done those inside. *The Burning Heart: Women Poets of Japan* (translations with Ikuko Atsumi) and *The Buddhist Writings of Lafcadio Hearn* (edited with Rexroth's introduction on Japanese Buddhism) followed in 1977; and *Seasons of Sacred Lust: Selected Poems of Kazuko Shiraishi* (translations of the most famous living woman poet of Japan done with Carol Tinker, Ikuko Atsumi, John Solt, and Yasuyo Morita) in 1978.

Also in 1978 the Rexroth's returned to Japan and toured South Korea, the Philippines, Hong Kong, Singapore, and Thailand, sponsored by the United States Agency of International Communication despite his outspoken objections to United States militarism and foreign policy; and a novelistic sequence of sixty short poems called *The Love Poems of Marichiko Translated by Kenneth Rexroth* and dedicated by him to her and by her to him proved that his passion was unflagging. The truth of the matter is that though he took pains to present these poems in public readings and in notes as translations, he confided to a few friends that he had made them up entirely himself. Staying in my home at Osaka University, he tried to produce, with the help of Yasuyo Morita and a young tanka poet, a full Japanese version of the poems to be published as Marichiko's original work, but was dissatisfied with the results, which were incomplete and never published, though some of the proceedings remain on a tape in my possession. The Marichiko poems were republished in 1979 in *The Morning Star*, containing also *The Silver Swan* and *On Flower Wreath Hill*. This last book of his original poetry, along with *Li Ch'ing Chao: Complete Poems* (translations of the greatest Chinese woman poet done with Ling Chung), were the last full books to be published in his lifetime as he faced death from a failing heart.[39]

In 1980, *For Rexroth*, edited by Geoffrey Gardner, the first Festschrift about his work, appeared as he returned to Japan for an international poetry conference despite declining health. That year Bradford Morrow issued a chapbook of Rexroth's light verse for his birthday, *Saucy Limericks and Christmas Cheer*, and the next year edited *Excerpts from a Life*, Rexroth's last publication that he was able to read. He was able to join in the celebration of his earlier career as an abstract painter at the retrospective show at the Santa Barbara Museum of Art.[40]

Although Rexroth had been baptised an Episcopalian, at his request his good friend Father Alberto Huerta, S.J., of the University of San Francisco, gave him a Roman Catholic baptism on Easter Sunday, 1981, and thereafter said Mass for him periodically at his bedside, where he was immobilized for over a year because of strokes and heart trouble. He was unable to speak at our last meeting, ten days before his death on 6 June 1982, but with tears in his eyes squeezed my hand in reply to questions. Courageous to the end, he had refused hospitalization; so James Laughlin had generously arranged for around-the-clock medical care at home, where Carol Tinker could remain with him. On 11 June an ecumenical funeral was conducted by four Jesuit priests at Our Lady of Mount Carmel Church near their home, with nuns from the Santa Barbara Vedanta temple chanting in Sanskrit, with music composed by his friend Dick Collins of the Dave Brubeck Quartet, and with the orientalist Esther Handler giving a reading of *On Flower Wreath Hill*. Father Huerta eloquently celebrated

> Rexroth's profound ability to contemplate the things which make up this universe: the leaves that descend down some river in the high Sierras in the Fall, the Japanese red sun that illuminates with a sudden flash at dawn in Kyoto, the mediterranean colors of Aix en Provence in Spring, or the simple rustling leaves and the infinite kaleidoscope sky which he contemplated with his sensitive blue eyes for over one year from his rectangular bedroom window. For when he could not speak, nor sit outside on the porch to let the light touch him, he would travel with his heart and mind through this opening in the wall to the incandescent light of all faith and all truth.

Rexroth was buried in the Santa Barbara cemetery, overlooking the Pacific Ocean, among cypresses and pines.[41]

John Solt, his former student and collaborator on translations, organized a memorial service at the Marishiten Temple in Tokyo the following August at which poet Kazuko Shiraishi and actress Maralia Yoshimasu read *The Love Poems of Marichiko* and sutras were chanted. In October, a memorial program of Rexroth's poems was led by poet-professor Yuzuru Katagiri, who read his Japanese translations of them at the Kyoto American Center and presented the eighth annual Rexroth Awards, which Rexroth had founded, to Japanese women. Memorial issues of *Kyoto Review*, *Seiza* (Tokyo), *Poetry Flash*, and *Sagetrieb* appeared. Katagiri's Japanese translations in 1978, 1979, and 1984 extended Rexroth's influence in Asia.[42] On 4 June 1983, a memorial poetry reading was held at the Kyoto American Center, led by Katagiri and involving poet-friends Nanao Sakaki, Yō Nakayama, and myself, with jazz accompaniment by Ron Hadley; and Keiko Matsui Gibson described him in a memorial poem as "a firey Buddha, a raging Fudo-Myoo" (a fierce-looking but compassionate king with upraised sword whose sculptured form guards Tantric Buddhist temples).[43] I also offered memorial lectures on Rexroth and Buddhism on five Japanese campuses, including Koya-san University in the awesome monastery which Rexroth had considered his spiritual home in Japan. In 1984 Brad Morrow's selection of Rexroth's poetry was published by New Directions.[44]

"Poetry Is Vision"—"Vision Is Love":
Rexroth's Philosophy of Literature

According to Rexroth's theory and practice, poetry is vision. Poets and critics have often used this term carelessly, but in Rexroth's work "vision" has several definite meanings that cohere in his organic philosophy of literature-in-community.

"Vision," referring to phases of a creative process of consciousness, sometimes means contemplation, in which the poet communed with nature and those he loved, and in which he periodically had oceanic, ecstatic experiences of realization, illumination, or enlightenment. At these times, sensation, perception, thinking, and feeling, especially love, were clarified, purified, and radically expanded; so he claimed that "vision is love."[1] As experience became intellectualized, vision came to mean the act of philosophizing and also the worldview projected by philosophizing; so vision is both sensuous and abstract, nonverbal and literary, personal and transpersonal. Rexroth's world vision is both conservative in reviving and uniquely synthesizing Hebraic-Christian, classical, Buddhist, and modern traditions of spiritual realization, and revolutionary in its vigorous opposition to the prevailing impersonality and alienation of modern society, technology, and culture. As Rexroth's personal experiences were expressed in poetry, vision became the act of poetic communication, evolving from interpersonal communion and recreating community. His vision is uniquely his, yet is also universal in scope and validity because it realizes the person in world community. Rexroth's world vision reveals his, and our, "Being in the World," as Heidegger put it.

"Poetry is vision," Rexroth asserts in "Poetry, Regeneration, and D. H. Lawrence," "the pure act of sensual communion and contemplation."[2] Does he mean all poetry, or the best of it? Obviously his idea is normative rather than descriptive, characterizing the poetry of Lawrence, Yeats, Blake, Whitman, poetry that he translated by Tu Fu, Li Ch'ing Chao, Sappho, Dante, and his own. He means by "vision" the essence of poetry, the quality that makes it true poetry, the quality often ignored by critics who emphasize form, structure, construction, or technique at the expense of imagination, or identify artifice as poetry itself. Craftsmanship is important in Rexroth's own poetry and all poetry that he values, but as a means to an end rather than as an end in itself. What, in his opinion, does poetry at its best communicate? Visionary experience: vision itself. And what is that?

He defines poetic vision as an *act*, a dynamic transformation of experience rather than as passive reflection; and it is a *pure* act, unlike impure acts of ordinary experience that lack unifying aesthetic concentration. There may be a suggestion that poetry is a purifying act, as in Aristotle's idea of catharsis; but in Rexroth's view poetry does more than purge impure emotions, for *communion* implies that poetry is an intimate experience of mutuality, a sacramental act of commemoration in which we may be mystically united with others and perhaps with reality as a whole. Such communion is *sensual*, for delightful sounds of language indicated by the artistry of calligraphy or typography evoke the imagined world of the poem. So poetry is a *contemplative* act, arising in deep, clear, open-minded, loving awareness. The text and form of the poem reveal the visionary act which is the essential poetry.

Rexroth shows that vision is organic consciousness, sympathetic, clear, and steady, communing, communicating, realizing the many in the one, the one in the many, the universality of each being. In vision, the observer is united with the observed, the poet communes directly with other beings, and all interact in community which extends through galaxies and transpersonal dimensions of mind that he called Buddha-worlds. Such thinking must be experienced in poetry itself, not abstracted from it as doctrine, just as in understanding music we must experience music musically.

Visionary experience—essentially formless—sometimes takes form; but *a* vision is not vision, as Rexroth carefully points out in *The Heart's Garden, The Garden's Heart*: "visions are/The measure of the defect/Of vision."[3] Because true vision is clarified interpersonal consciousness, not hallucination, dream, or fantasy, Rexroth's poetics is opposed to surrealism and dada, as shown in his cubist poem, "Fundamental Disagreement with Two Contemporaries," which alludes to Tristan Tzara and André Breton.[4] Similarly, Rexroth refused to identify true vision with the drug highs of the Beat generation, for he doubted that Allen Ginsberg's and Jack Kerouac's frantic searches for vision in *Howl* and *On the Road* got them beyond confusion. According to Rexroth, vision is habitual clear-mindedness:

> The illuminated live
> Always in light and so do
> Not know it is there as fishes
> Do not know they live in water.[5]
> . . . .
> St. John of the Cross said it,
> The desire for vision is
> The sin of gluttony.[6]

"The True Person"

Rexroth insisted that vision is personal, the experience of a "true person" in community. "The universalization of the human soul, the creation of the true person," was evident in the life of Albert Schweitzer, for example.[7] Such a person is neither merely a self-made man, nor someone who simply loses himself in work or meditation. He or she loses ego, but not the whole person, which is realized in creative interaction with others. Rexroth takes himself for granted as an integral person instead of condemning himself as a sinner or striving to change himself into someone else.

Rexroth's personalism is aesthetic as well as ethical and psychological. Because vision is personal, he typically stands undisguised in his poetry and prose instead of concealing himself behind an impersonal literary construction, a mask, like Yeats, or an "objective correlative," like Eliot and the New Critics. Rexroth's poetic theory and most of his practice challenge the impersonality of much modernist literature and criticism, particularly as Eliot dogmatized in "Tradition and the Individual Talent" about the necessity of the poet's losing his personality as he learns to express not himself but his medium. Rexroth's "progress" as poet was radically subversive of Eliot's principles, for Rexroth's work was a continual revelation of personality, his own and the personalities of the many poets from many cultures whose work he translated after imaginatively conversing with them. He might have argued against James Joyce's Stephen Dedalus that the true poet remains in his handiwork like a pantheistic god, instead of invisibly behind it like the god of Roman Catholicism. Rexroth openly participates in much of his poetry, excepting his plays, and even in them the characters' tragic lives dramatize the poet's philosophical personalism, which links each one with the fate of the human race, as the chorus proclaims near the end of *Beyond the Mountains*:

> There are countless
> Iphigenias marching to
> Their deaths at this moment in all
> The dust motes of the rising sun.
>
> There are no things in the real
> World. Only persons have being.
> Things are perspectives on persons—
> A mote of dust is a distant
> Person seen with dusty interest.[8]

Communion: "Communication Raised to the Highest Power"

Rexroth's poetry typically arises out of preverbal, preconceptual, visionary experiences similar to those described in the sutras and tantras, D. T. Suzuki's Zen writings, William James's *Varieties of Religious Experience*, Martin Buber's *I and Thou*, Jacob Boehme's *The Signature of All Things*, George Fox's *Journals*, Vedanta, and other sources referred to throughout his work; but he remained skeptical of dogmatic and theoretical explanations, especially those depending upon an Absolute or a supernatural god. His sense that "The Holy is in the heap of dust—it is the heap of dust"[9] was no different from the Quaker Inner Light, Blake's "Heaven in a wild flower," the emptiness of the Buddha-nature, but such an intuition cannot be forced into a dogmatic system, for such experience can only be intimated artistically, not defined scientifically.

Rexroth's "perfect communion with others"[10] was often erotic, but at the same time it transcended physical attraction. In his many love poems, the women are spiritual beings, sometimes human, sometimes divine, as in the seventeenth poem of *The Silver Swan*, when, before dawn in Japan, he imagines a nude girl taking form from the light of the Morning Star: "her/Body flows into mine, each/Corpuscle of light merges/With a corpuscle of blood or flesh."[11] But the erotic mysticism that permeates his poetry is but one kind of communion and, as we learn from his introduction to *The Phoenix and the Tortoise*, it is but a phase in the development of the person out of despair, through sacramental marriage, to a realization of universal responsibility.[12] With this responsibility, a person acts with compassionate consciousness of world community. So communion of two persons in the "mutual being" of love entails, by implication, responsibility for all beings in universal community; for each is inseparable from all.

In regarding poetry as vision, Rexroth meant that it arises out of contemplation and communion to become communication and so was not complete as merely private experience. So he can also, without contradiction, say that poetry is "interpersonal communication raised to the highest power."[13] "It communicates the most intense experiences of very highly developed sensibilities," he wrote in one of his most important essays on aesthetics, "Unacknowledged Legislators and Art pour Art," in which he emphasized the personal origin of poetry and its communication not predominantly of feeling or thought, but of whole experiences: "A love poem is an act of communication of love, like a kiss."[14] Such communication has a strong ethical value, strangely reminiscent of Matthew Arnold's "criticism of life"; or in Rexroth's words "symbolic criticism of values."[15] So love poems and nature poems become criticisms of a dehumanized culture based on the alienation of people from one another, from their own nature, and from the universe as a whole. But such moral and intellectual functions of poetry are never separated from its emotional, psychological, sensuous, and spiritual aspects, for it "widens and deepens and sharpens the sensibility."[16]

Rexroth felt that Chinese and Japanese poetry often communicates experiences of such "highly developed sensibilities" more directly and purely than most European poetry because "Most poetry in the Western world is more or less corrupted with rhetoric and manipulation . . . with program and exposition, and the actual poetry, the living speech of person to person, has been a by product."[17] This extraordinary statement, which might well be debated, may suggest one reason for Rexroth's turn from cubism, prevalent in his theory and practice of poetry as well as painting between the World Wars, to the poetry of natural speech, which became his predominant mode from *The Phoenix and the Tortoise* (1944) on. Also, terms from European and American philosophy and historical struggles, so prominent in his poetry before *The Heart's Garden, The Garden's Heart* (1967), were used less often as oriental and especially Buddhist themes and imagery filled his poetry, both original work and translations.

In Rexroth's view, communication rests upon some preunderstanding from communion and community. A message is not transmitted mechanically by means of a text, from sender to receiver; rather, meaning evolves from preestablished community, some kind of mutual existence and mutual interest. Out of I-Thou, meaning comes. Unless we share consciousness, we can understand nothing. True communication, through poetry and other arts, helps us realize mutual being.

"The Craft Is the Vision and the Vision Is the Craft"

In emphasizing vision, Rexroth may seem to underplay skill; but in fact he was a meticulous craftsman in both poetry and prose, and his criticism of literature places a high premium on artistic technique, not as an end in itself as in aestheticism, but as a means of communicating experience. He appreciated subtle forms and techniques of many kinds of art such as action painting, progressive jazz, and the Revolution of the Word that were often condemned as obscure; but they moved him because of his sensitivity to craftsmanship and his curiosity about its meaning. "Purposive construction of any kind is a species of communication," he wrote, "just as any kind of communication must be structured."[18] And in successful visionary poetry such as Lawrence's *Birds, Beasts, and Flowers*, "the craft is the vision and the vision is the craft."[19]

Rexroth's own craftsmanship is impressive, and his prosody

deserves a long study. He wrote some rhymed quatrains and limericks as well as a few unpublished sonnets, but most of his poetry is in free verse and in syllabic patterns that are intricately melodious; for example, the nine-syllable lines of most of *The Homestead Called Damascus*, the 7 to 8 syllable lines of most of *The Dragon and the Unicorn*, *The Heart's Garden*, *The Garden's Heart*, and of parts of *Beyond the Mountains*, and the seven syllable lines of many shorter poems such "The Reflecting Trees of Being and Not Being":

> In my childhood when I first
> Saw myself unfolded in
> The triple mirrors, in my
> Youth, when I pursued myself
> Wandering on wandering
> Nightbound roads like a roving
> Masterless dog, when I met
> Myself on sharp peaks of ice.
> And tasted myself dissolved
> In the lulling heavy sea,
> In the talking night, in the
> Spiraling stars, what did I
> Know?[20]

If this passage is read aloud so that the seven syllables of each line are given equal duration, sound and meaning are fused with great clarity and dignity. Syllabic verse seems eminently suited for Rexroth's poetics of visionary communication in that it focuses attention directly on sound's meaning, the sense of sense, with more control than free verse because of regular line-lengths, whereas rhymed and accentually metered verse divides attention between the abstract sound system and the actual sound and meaning of language. In transmitting experience with maximum directness, Rexroth did not want the playful tension between abstract and actual patterns of sound, which are appropriately enriching in other kinds of poetry. He seems to have been influenced by syllabic verse in Japanese, Chinese, and French, which he translated profusely, more than by contemporary practitioners of syllabics in English such as W. H. Auden, Marianne Moore, and Dylan Thomas. Why he chose to write lines of certain length is not certain, but they feel normal in English, in which we are accustomed to alternating lines in ballad stanzas of eight syllables (not counting truncations and other frequent variations) and in most poems before free verse, pentameter lines of ten syllables: Rexroth seems to have discovered natural line-lengths from seven to nine syllables without regular accentual patterns. The seven-syllable lines (mixed with five-syllable lines) of Japanese haiku and tanka also influenced his practice. The framework of seven syllables, in this poem, allows for full freedom of speech, while at the same time providing emphases at the ends and beginnings of lines—"first," "Saw," "Youth," "myself," "Wandering" (repeated), "Nightbound," "roving," "Masterless," "Myself," "ice," "dissolved," "sea," "Spiraling," "I," and "Know."

There are also profuse echoes from line to line, supporting the unrolling theme, in parallelism indicated in the following diagram:

> In my childhood
> > when I first / Saw myself
> > > unfolded in / The triple mirrors
> in my / Youth
> > when I pursued myself /
> > > Wandering on wandering /
> > > > Nightbound roads
> > > > > like a roving / Masterless dog,
> > when I met / Myself
> > > on sharp peaks of ice, /
> > And tasted myself
> > > dissolved /
> > > > In the lulling heavy sea, /
> > > > In the talking night,
> > > > In the / Spiraling stars,
> what did I / Know?

This subtly constructed poem of cosmic vision continues with his questioning what he knows now, as he imagines his blood flowing out to the nebulas and back. Losing himself in the vastness of the universe, he knows only faces of other persons, mostly of his beloved, beyond space and time.

Rexroth explained how he deliberately patterned vowels and consonants to enhance the melody of much of his verse, a method that he seems to have learned in part from Japanese poetry:

Most of these poems are in syllabic lines. (Sometimes after the poem is cast in syllabic lines it is broken up into cadences.) Against this is counterpointed a rhythm primarily of quantity, secondarily of accent. In addition, close attention is paid to the melodic line of the vowels and to the evolution of consonants (p–b–k, m–r–l–y, *etc.*). In most cases a melody was written at the time of the poem.[21]

What is important here is that the melody is inherent in the poem's language, in the rise and fall of pitch in the spoken poem, rather than being determined by an abstract form imposed upon natural speech.

Indeed, Rexroth's poetry is most often in the direct statement and address of "natural numbers," in the normal grammar of actual speech. Symbolism characterizes *The Homestead Called Damascus*, his first long poem written between 1920 and 1925, but this mode was then abandoned. A third mode, described by Rexroth as cubism or objectivism, was practiced mostly between the World Wars, with such work collected chiefly in the latter half of *In What Hour* (1940) and *The Art of Worldly Wisdom* (1940), though some also appears later.

The Vicarity of Symbolism

In his youth, Rexroth wrote symbolist poetry which evolved into *The Homestead Called Damascus*, his first long philosophical poem. This musical narrative of the traumatic quests of two brothers is full of symbols and myths of decadence, sacrifice, and fertility—a rambling home full of the bric-a-brac of imperialism; dreams of Tammuz and Adonis, castrated; Persephone and a black stripper promising sexual-spiritual revitalization. The brothers have vague, inconclusive, meandering metaphysical and theological conversations and helpless fantasies about a beautiful Renaissance maiden who occasionally rides past on a white horse. The poem echoes Stevens, Yeats, Aiken, Proust, James, French symbolist poets, anthropological scholars such as Frazer, Weston, Harrison, Cornford, Murray; and the strongest influence of all, Eliot, whose *The Waste Land* had enthused Rexroth until he realized that Eliot stood against everything that he was working for.[22] The style of *Homestead* was not compatible with Rexroth's emerging aesthetic theory and practice of cubism and later of direct utterance, so he wrote nothing else like it and did not publish it for thirty years. Moreover, symbolism, suggesting a transcendent reality remote from immediate experience, grew from a metaphysic opposite to his idea of immanence, that the "Holy is the heap of dust" and is not symbolized by it. Nevertheless, the poem is a remarkable achievement that deserves to be honored for its own sake, for the sensuousness of its sound, the complexity of its characters and their interactions, the suggestiveness of its imagery, and its philosophical implications:

> I know this is an ambivalent
> Vicarity—who stands for who?
> And this is the reality then—
> This flesh, the flesh of this arm and I
> Know how this flesh lies on this bone
> Of this arm, this is reality—
> I know. I ask nothing more of it.
> These things are beautiful, these are
> My sacraments and I ask no more.[23]

The Revolution of the Word: Cubism and Objectivism

Rexroth's cubist poetry and painting launched him into the international avant-garde between the two World Wars, when the Revolution of the Word was in full swing.[24] It was a comprehensive revolution, not only of language, but also of the mind and of life itself. Whereas symbolist poetry seemed to be a language of aristocratic decadence, cubism appealed to his ambition to reconstruct language along with everything else. His youthful, elitist commitment to change the world was lifelong, though his modes of writing changed.[25]

Rexroth's earliest cubist poems were written as early as 1920, but were not published in little magazines after 1929 and were not collected until 1949, when they appeared in *The Art of Worldly Wisdom*, including, along with short poems, *A Prolegomenon to a Theodicy*. Such writing was called "objectivist," but he preferred to describe his work as cubist, involving "the analysis of reality into simple units and the synthesis of the work of art as a real parallel to experience," as in Eisenstein's films, some of the poetry of

Apollinaire, Cocteau, Cendrars, MacOrlan, Deltier, Soupault, Aragon, Tzara, Eluard, and especially Reverdy in France, Williams, Pound, Stein, Winters, Arensberg, Lowenfels, and Zukofsky in America, songs of preliterate people such as American Indians, and of course cubist painting.[26]

Rexroth vigorously and originally promoted the cubist aesthetic, theoretically and practically, in his own paintings, poems, essays, and translations from the French. His analytical mind was attracted to the direct, definite reconstruction of experience as an art object, which he distinguished from the dreamy suggestiveness of symbolism and surrealism. "In the Memory of Andrée Rexroth," the agonizing elegy opening *The Art of Worldly Wisdom*, is Rexroth's cubism at its best, at once personal and objective:

> is a question of mutual being
> a question of congruence or
> proximity a question of
> a sudden passage in air beyond
> a window a long controlled fall
> of music . . . [27]

Rexroth's introduction to Reverdy contains his strongest defense of cubism, which as a young man he was sure would be the future of American poetry: "Its revolution is aimed at the syntax of the mind itself."[28] Such poetry, he claims, induces in the reader

> Vertigo, rapture, transport, crystalline and plangent
> sounds, shattered and refracted light, indefinite depth,
> weightlessness, piercing odors and tastes, and synthesizing
> the sensations and affects, an all-consuming clarity.[29]

This claim cannot be argued, but only tested in the actual experience of reading cubist poetry—such as, for example, the last section of "Andromeda Chained to Her Rock the Great Nebula in Her Heart":

> Eyes in moss
> Salt in mouth
> Stone in heart
> An owl rings the changes of silence
> Torn head
> Crow's wings
> Black eyeballs

Poison seeps through the parabolic sand
The rock on fire
Ice falls towards the sun[30]

Reading such a passage, I experience vertigo and some of the extreme sense impressions described by Rexroth, but not, I regret to say, an "all-consuming clarity," which more aptly characterizes the poems in "natural numbers" rather than cubist poems. The phenomena that he describes are comparable to those of mystical experiences; but he is careful to make a fundamental distinction between religious experiences, which are "necessitated and ultimate," and visionary poems, which are not.[31] Poetry may communicate vision in the sense of communion, I-Thou, without being itself *a* vision of transcendent being.

Why did Rexroth turn away from cubism after it had made him internationally famous? In the 1953 preface to *The Art of Worldly Wisdom*, he explains that because even some of his friends in the avant-garde did not comprehend his cubist poems, he decided to reach a wider community of readers by writing very much as he spoke, in normal syntax. Nevertheless, some cubist poems continued to appear even in his late books, in the section called "Gödel's Proof" at the outset of *The Collected Shorter Poems*, for example. He never gave up on cubism, helping to revive it in essays and translations of French poetry.

Though not much in favor today, Rexroth's cubist poetry nevertheless shows his early artistic originality, his immense intellectual power, and his contribution to a worldwide cultural transformation that continues today in "language poetry" and other manifestations. In practicing cubism, he analyzed and controlled the elements of language in innovative ways that carried over to "natural numbers," especially in startling juxtapositions of particulars of experience and the phrasings of direct address. Whenever in later years he returned to cubism in his poetry, translations, and essays, it was a reminder that the Revolution of the Word and of Life had not been extinguished, even during the repressiveness of the cold war.

"Natural Numbers"—"Striving to Write the Way I Talk"

Rexroth's most characteristic, successful, and popular mode of poetic communication might be called "natural numbers," a term used in the title of one of his books, referring to poetry that stylistically approximates, in syntax and diction, actual speech of person to person. From about 1920 on he wrote translations from Greek, Chinese, Japanese, and Latin in this mode, starting with translations of Sappho:

> . . . about the cool water
> the wind sounds through sprays
> of apple, and from the quivering leaves
> slumber pours down . . . [32]

The classical directness and clarity of ancient poetry, especially of Japanese tanka, mastered through the art of translations, infused his original poems as well. Among the earliest of these is the sequence for Leslie Smith entitled "The Thin Edge of Your Pride," dated 1922–1926, containing such perfect imagist passages as:

> After an hour the mild
> Confusion of snow
> Amongst the lamplights
> Has softened and subdued
> The nervous lines of bare
> Branches etched against
> The chill twilight. [33]

Rexroth had become famous as a cubist before the poems in "natural numbers" began appearing in periodicals in the mid-1930s. He speaks through the "natural" poems as if a listener is present, so the poems are intense, dramatic speech-acts, typically expressing love or friendship, often grief, sometimes outrage and social protest. Even if a listener does not seem to be present, in poems of meditation and lone reminiscence, for instance, the voice remains so intimate that the reader becomes Rexroth's *confidant*. In autobiographical poems such as "A Living Pearl" and contemplative poems in the mountains such as "Lyell's Hypothesis Again" and "Toward an Organic Philosophy," the words draw us toward him as if we are sitting beside a campfire under the stars, listening to him talk. [34]

Direct address is also evident in the revolutionary rhetoric of the poems in the first half of *In What Hour*, the antiwar memorial for Dylan Thomas called "Thou Shalt Not Kill," the ethical speculations of *The Dragon and the Unicorn*, and the dramatic tetralogy *Beyond the*

Mountains, stylistically influenced by Japanese No drama. "I have spent my life striving to write the way I talk," Rexroth wrote,[35] and his public readings convincingly demonstrated the relationship between his writing and speaking. Even when technical terms from the sciences, philosophy, politics, and theology enter his prose and poetry, along with literary and historical allusions from the major civilizations, there is a natural flow of living speech, an acceptance of the Tao, the way things naturally are, except in the symbolist and cubist poems, in which language has been willfully, sometimes forcefully, reconstructed. "Natural numbers" became the appropriate mode for the Buddhist worldview that grew in importance in Rexroth's work from World War II on, for in Buddhism, the will and ego turn out to be illusions floating in calm, compassionate contemplation.

"Actual Poetry Is the Living Speech of Person to Person"

The evolution of Rexroth's chief poetic mode, "natural numbers," from lyrical, elegiac, and satirical to dramatic forms, supported and was supported by his idea that "actual poetry is the living speech of person to person."[36] His friend William Carlos Williams, with whom he had many affinities, believed that "you have no other speech than poetry"[37]; and Whitman had heard America singing in its common speech. Rexroth thought that poems are derived from the poetic flow of living speech, that poems are realized orally, that texts like scores of music are indications of oral performance, an art which he practiced and promoted extensively long before readings became commonplace. Through this process, poetry unites poet and audience in community. This approach counteracts the pedantic idea that poetry is fundamentally on the page or in the mind as an object of impersonal analytical study, or that poetry is some kind of artificially constructed arrangement of words that no one would ever conceivably say to one another. For Rexroth, true poetry realizes the spiritual union of Martin Buber's I-Thou.[38]

Not all actual speech can be poetry, of course, for much talk is thoroughly debased; but poetry cannot be poetry unless it is vital communication from sensibility to sensibility, actualized in speech from one to another. The idea would have been readily accepted by the ancient Greeks, Chinese, and Japanese, among others who thought of poetry as song that unites performers and audience.

When Rexroth implies that poetic communication depends on sensibility, he seems dependent on Wordsworth, who defined a poet as "a man speaking to men—a man, it is true, endowed with more lively sensibility, more enthusiasm and tenderness, who has greater knowledge of human nature, and a more comprehensive soul, than are supposed to be common among mankind."[39] Despite this fundamental agreement about the poet's nature and function, however, there are differences of emphasis; for whereas sensibility for Wordsworth is innately endowed, for Rexroth it can be developed to the qualitative magnitude necessary for true poetry: so poets may be made as well as born.

Poetry as Communal Sacrament

According to Rexroth, poetry originates in personal vision (communion with others), takes form in the direct communication of living speech, person-to-person, and functions sacramentally in community. In "American Indian Songs" he shows how song, and art generally, unite the individual to society and nature.[40] People alienated from nature, from each other, and from themselves, as most people are in modern secular, industrial or postindustrial society, cannot imagine living organically; so poetry has a revolutionary function in reminding us that we *do* live in nature, in some kind of community, invaded and broken though it may be by technological forces that divide us from each other. In *An Autobiographical Novel* Rexroth wrote eloquently about the sacramental activities of organic societies:

> In the rites of passage—the fundamental activities and relationships of life—birth, death, sexual intercourse, eating, drinking, choosing a vocation, adolescence, mortal illness—life at its important moments is ennobled by the ceremonious introduction of transcendence: the universe is focused on the event in a Mass or ceremony that is itself a kind of dance and a work of art.[41]

He centered on his own rites of passage and those of his family: his birth, sexual and intellectual awakenings of adolescence, his parents' illnesses and deaths, hopes for a religious vocation that climaxed during a retreat in an Anglo-Catholic monastery, and his lifelong commitment to the vocations of poet, artist and revolutionary.[42] He wrote to and about his children and their growing awareness of the universe in "The Lights in the Sky Are Stars," "Mary and the Seasons," "Xmas Coming," and many other poems.[43] He heartrendingly commemorated his mother in two elegies and his first wife Andrée in three elegies.[44] Some of his most intensely erotic poems are the Marichiko poems.[45] Eating and drinking are celebrated in several appetizing passages in *The Dragon and the Unicorn*[46] and elsewhere. Countless nature poems center on ritualistic observations of seasonal cycles and the motions of heavenly bodies.

Of all rites of passage, Rexroth seems to have been most preoccupied with marriage, for his spiritual aim was to move

> from abandon to erotic mysticism, from erotic mysticism to the ethical mysticism of sacramental marriage, thence to the realization of the ethical mysticism of universal responsibility . . . [47]

In sacramental marriage as distinct from a merely legal bond, the I-Thou of interpersonal communion (the original vision of poetry) is realized and celebrated as the center of community, uniting each person with humanity as a whole, in universal responsibility. The union of the loving couple is the nexus of the mystical union of all. The theme is prominent in *The Phoenix and the Tortoise*, the Marichiko poems, and many others.

Rexroth's poetry is typically sacramental whether it celebrates erotic and marital union or processes of nature, humanistic revolts for freedom, or visionary creations. His poetry as a whole transmits a boundless reverence for life and love of humanity.

Most comprehensively of all the shorter poems "A Letter to William Carlos Williams" reveals Rexroth's visionary poetics, his commitment to poetry as interpersonal communion, communication of vision, and communal sacrament. In intimate direct address, Rexroth compares Williams to St. Francis, Brother Juniper, and Yeats's Fool of wisdom and beauty. He praises Williams's quiet affection for red wheelbarrows, cold plums, Queen Anne's lace; his stillness like that of George Fox and Christ, from which the authentic speech of poetry emerged. Then Rexroth prophesies that a young woman, walking one day in a utopian landscape by "the lucid Williams River," will tell her children that it used to be the polluted Passaic in the Dark Ages; and just as the river flows through nature, Williams's veins, Rexroth's speech, history, the imagined woman and her children, as well as those of us who read the poem—flowing like the Tao, the Way of Lao-tzu—so all participate in the universal community of all beings, revealed in poetry:

> And that is what a poet
> Is, children, one who creates
> Sacramental relationships
> That last always.[48]

The Poems

So busy was Rexroth being a totally committed cultural revolutionary—polemicist, critic, activist, translator, painter, and playwright as well as poet—that he was thirty-four before his first book appeared and sixty before *The Collected Shorter Poems* came out in the mid-1960s. By then, his erotic-mystical, anarchistic-ecological, prophetic worldview seemed to be finding fulfillment in worldwide countercultural movements for liberation from political, artistic, and sexual repression, but he doubted that the human race or the planet could be saved. Giving up on western civilization, he found the equanimity of compassionate realization in the Buddhist tradition, which had hitherto played an important but subordinate role in his work. His first tour of Asia in 1967, with the publication of *The Heart's Garden, The Garden's Heart* that year and *The Collected Longer Poems* the next, initiated the final phase of his work. Subsequent poems, nearly all evolving from Japanese experiences, were collected in *New Poems* in 1974 and *The Morning Star* in 1979.

The Collected Shorter Poems (1966)

"Gödel's Proof" (1965)

In *The Collected Shorter Poems*, a section of new poems called "Gödel's Proof" precedes work from seven previously published books. Like the mathematician who proved that "A self-contained system is a contradiction in terms. QED" (quoted as an epigraph), Rexroth withdrew from efforts to construct a unified philosophy, which since his adolescence had been countered by skepticism on the one hand and visionary experience on the other. The second epigraph, his translation of the anonymous Provençal nightingale poem more famously rendered by Pound, affirms the way of love and nature.[1]

After a burst of desperate dissociation, Rexroth celebrates erotic joy in the jazzy cadences of "Travelers in Erewhon" (*CSP*, 6) and other free verses in direct statement which he loved to recite to music. Sensuousness ranges from the lowlife simplicity of "Oaxaca 1925" (*CSP*, 7) to the elegance of "High Provence" (*CSP*, 9). He seems to have aged into a second youth, recalling his first. Each fleeting mortal instant is lived fully, for its own sake, as he swings through cycles of despair, love, separation, and loneliness—most vividly, perhaps, in the sequence called "Time Is an Inclusion Series Said McTaggart" (*CSP*, 12–13). Light, heat, snow, fog, and water envelop him and his loved ones as they dissolve in nature (*CSP*, 6, 7, 10, 19). In such a fertile atmosphere, the cubist poems in "Gödel's Proof" seem strained and out of place; but in the more natural poems, affection embraces daughters, wife, and all of nature until he suddenly agonizes over mistaken love in an allusion to divorce (*CSP*, 22).

What can be depended upon? Only the cycles of nature, shown in "Yin and Yang," the last original poem in "Gödel's Proof" before a few Chinese translations (*CSP*, 23):

> The flowers are back in their places.
> The birds back in their usual trees.
> The winter stars set in the ocean.
> The summer stars rise from the mountains.
> The air is filled with atoms of quicksilver.
> Resurrection envelops the earth.

In this most liturgical and cyclic of all Rexroth's poems, the language flows effortlessly and archetypes harmoniously balance. Moving from Leo to Virgo, the moon fertilizes the virgin, who holds in moonlight the symbolic wheat of the Eleusinian mysteries, while under the world the sun moves through Pisces, the double fish and the Chinese symbol of Yin/Yang, dark/light, female/male, passive/active, and so on.

All but three lines of the poem have nine syllables, with the eleven of "The air is filled with atoms of quicksilver" quickening the pace. The last two lines of the poem, having eight syllables each, are slower, more gnomic, and statelier than the others: "In the underworld the sun swims/Between the fish called Yes and No." Emerging from the syllabic movement, however, is a triple accentual pattern in the lines about flowers, birds, winter, and summer stars, the most emphatic being "The lion gives the moon to the virgin./She stands at the crossroads of heaven." A dactyllic movement in other lines such as these supports the prophetic tone so firmly that the poem could be sung as a sacred hymn. The melody begins with short *i*'s, then opens into long *o*'s, *a*'s and *u*'s which pass through subtle variations in relation to neighboring consonants: from *spring* to *range*, from *warm* to *perfumed*, from *under* to *Easter moon*, on an underlying stream of sibilants. Changes of pace are also effective in this poem, beginning as it does with the languid "It is spring once more in the Coast Range," then quickening with the sharp accents of the next lines of emphatic parallelism, but slowing in the last two lines.

The tender anguish of the new poems is intensified by the theme that no instant can be redeemed. All passes away. Flowers, birds, and stars return, but they are never the same, and we are never the same. Even if patterns are eternal, particular experiences never are. In "The Wheel Revolves" Rexroth's daughter reincarnates the dancer immortalized by Po Chu I; and as summer and swallows return to the mountains where they are camping, "Ten thousand years revolve without change./All this will never be again" (*CSP*, 21). Faith in creation cannot save the particular day, or daughter, from mutability. Having passed through countless cycles of despair, ecstacy, matrimonial responsibility, and disillusionment, Rexroth returns to a "rite of rebirth" in nature and art.

The Art of Worldly Wisdom (1949 and 1953): 1920–1932

Turning back from the aging bard to the precocious innovator of *The Art of Worldly Wisdom*, included next in part in *CSP* (with "A Prolegomenon to a Theodicy" appearing in *CLP*), we are struck by the persistent anguish of mutability, the perennial loss of love, the mature awareness of death from the beginning of Rexroth's work. The stylistic and intellectual complexities of his earliest poems, written between the ages of fifteen and twenty-seven, do not obscure the fear and trembling of a youthful struggle for light out of darkness.

After Rexroth's most poignant cubist elegy, "In the Memory of Andrée Rexroth" (*CSP*, 27–30), "The Thin Edge of Your Pride 1922–26," a sequence of fourteen delicate love poems for Leslie Smith (*CSP*, 31–36) similar in style and tone to "Time Is an Inclusion Series Said McTaggart," opens with the colorful music of "Later when the gloated water/Burst with red lotus" that echoes Stevens and Tennyson, and ends with tankalike lines (*CSP*, 36):

> You alone,
> A white robe over your naked body,
> Passing and repassing
> Through the dreams of twenty years.

The eleven poems of a section called "Interoffice Communications" in the 1949 volume (arranged in *CSP*, 37–68), include "Phronesis" (meaning "practical wisdom," *CSP*, 37–40) and other cubist poems of agonizing syntax and despair that is relieved by the imagist love poem in plain speech beginning, "I pass your home in a slow vermilion dawn" (*CSP*, 47). The extended finale, "When You Asked for It" (*CSP*, 69–78), is the least obscure example of cubism in the collection because the elements of experience and language are more recognizable, as in the voice of one of the poor women: "I saw my sister in a white nightgown walking among purple tree trunks in a heavy fog very slow and with a gentle smile just like she was laid away."

The book is provocative, anguished, full of life and consciousness of death, intensified by advanced artistry but troublesome: a collection showing Rexroth's promising range of intellect and imagination, but not as satifying as his later work.

In What Hour (1940)

The thirty-one poems of *In What Hour*, written between the two World Wars, pose a metaphysical problem in that actuality "might have been otherwise," as Alfred North Whitehead observes in the epigraph (*CSP*, 79). The "otherwise" for Rexroth is revolutionary hope for a world community based on creativity, mutual aid, and love rather than on competition, coercion, exploitation, and war. But hope dimmed because of a pattern of historical defeats.

Recalling the brutal destruction of the Paris Commune in 1871, the Bolsheviks' massacre of the Kronstadt sailors in 1921 and other totalitarian perversions of revolutionary idealism, Fascist victories in Italy, Germany, and Spain, suppression of strikes and radicals in the United States, and the outbreak of World War II, Rexroth comes to view history as a tragic process in which values fall from heroic sacrifices. In these poems he is not in immediate danger, but above the battle, typically mountain-climbing in the Sierras, contemplating seasonal cycles of constellations, wildlife, and vast geological processes against which human struggles seem pitiful and terrible. The tragedy of history is viewed against the inevitable cycles of nature. The poems in the first half of the volume are generally in the style of direct address, vitally descriptive of nature and human conflict, often muscularly rhetorical, whereas poems in the second half transcend history to reveal "value in mountains" (*CSP*, 120) in a more detached cubist style.

In "Hiking on the Coast Range," the opening poem, blood from the stab of a wasp, reminding the poet of strikers killed in San Francisco, symbolizes the sacrificial creation of values (*CSP*, 84). Prophetic voices rise from the blood of social change in "From the Paris Commune to the Kronstadt Rebellion" (*CSP*, 81, entitled "March 18, 1871–1921" in the 1940 edition) and "The Motto on the Sundial" (*CSP*, 188); but if these warnings go unheeded, if the dream of freedom dies, then suicide would be seductive ("Gentlemen, I Address You Publicly," *CSP*, 83) and defeat would be inevitable ("At Lake Desolation," *CSP*, 82, in which regiments, their throats cut, are plowed under). In the face of world crisis, aestheticism is satirized in a parody of Auden's postcommunist conventionalities of playing safe, advising children to weave chains of violets instead of exploring the dangerous ruins of history (*CSP*, 85), and also in "A Very Early Morning Exercise," in which a decadent Chinese official mutters pretty poems (*CSP*, 91–92) in contrast to the courageous Tu Fu (Rexroth's favorite lyric poet), who hated despotism and war so much that he told off the Emperor ("Another Early Morning Exercise," *CSP*, 92–93). Rexroth never escapes into pure art or nature, for in "Autumn in California," for instance, as he wanders in idyllic weather, he imagines a Chinese mother bursting from a bomb and Spanish comrades conversing philosophically before battle (*CSP*, 94). Though admiring humane revolutionaries, he questions the illusory nature of action, which always eludes theory; for even as logical men with just intentions plan the future, real activists bungle and pervert such ideals ("New Objectives, New Cadres," *CSP*, 96). Only in nature can history be transcended. In "Requiem for the Spanish Dead," constellations offer cosmic solace during the Spanish Civil War (*CSP*, 86–87).

Two of Rexroth's periodic commemorations of the execution of Sacco and Vanzetti are "Climbing Milestone Mountain, August 22, 1937," in which he predicts that the peak will one day be named after them (*CSP*, 89–90), and "August 22, 1939," his finest poem on the social function of poetry (*CSP*, 97–99). Beginning with a passage from Sacco's final letter to his son Dante, the latter poem asks, "What is it all for, this poetry?"—"this alphabet of one sensibility?" The answer is that poetry reveals mysteries of nature, personality, love, death: "Values fall from history like men from shellfire." He prophesies that "The rule of iron and spilled blood" will at last give way to "The abiding solidarity of living blood and brain." Even as liberators are condemned to die, classic revolutionary slogans ring out hope:

> "Liberty is the mother
> Not the daughter of order."
> "Not the government of men
> But the administration of things."
> "From each according to his ability,
> Unto each according to his needs."

So history interweaves with nature. In "North Palisades, the End of September, 1939," he imagines peace beyond military victories (*CSP*, 100). "Towards an Organic Philosophy" (an allusion to Whitehead) shows in meticulous detail "The chain of dependence that runs through creation" (quoted from the naturalist Tyndall, *CSP*, 101). This ecological theme runs through many poems: his lover's eyes are the "color of snow" (*CSP*, 112); he remembers hearing his first grosbeak on a farm that has become a polluted suburb (*CSP*, 108); a girl, mountain-climbing with him, envisions a sunset on Saturn (*CSP*, 87); and in 1939 he watches moonlight on snow as war begins in Europe (*CSP*, 109).

Some atypical Renaissance influences show up briefly in "A Letter to Yvor Winters," metaphysically presenting "thin imagos that abide decay" out of "clouds of unknowing" (*CSP*, 104), and in love poems for Marie, whom he married after Andrée had died in 1940 (*CSP*, 105–107).

The last seven poems depart from the direct speech of "natural numbers." In "The Apple Garths of Avalon," resembling the symbolism of *Homestead*, Sebastian, one of the Damascan brothers, moves from aesthetic detachment into the absurd plethora of existence (*CSP*, 110–12). The cubist "Value in Mountains" (*CSP*, 120–22), taking off from Marx's theories of class struggle and surplus value, then moves from social to individual being and value. Asserting that "value is a food and not a weapon," he turns to the dialectic of mental creation in Part 2. In the last part of this poem, the style of shamanistic chanting should be compared with the sophisticated vocabulary in similar form, in "Easy Lessons in Geophagy" (*CSP*, 123). Both primitive and sophisticated techniques blend harmoniously in "A Lesson in Geography" (*CSP*, 129), which sounds more like Rexroth speaking than do the previous cubist poems, and which ends in ecological communion as he lies speaking and listening to stone that seems to be himself.

The final poem in the collection, "Ice Shall Cover Nineveh" (*CSP*, 130–36), is more explicitly prophetic than the other Cubist poems in this volume. The title alludes to a legend that the Gurgler Glacier once covered Nineveh because its citizens did not feed a hungry pilgrim who was said to be one of the Magi. The calm of mountain solitude is broken by the thought of the inevitability of death for both individuals and civilizations. In trying to make sense of such loss, the poet recommends the kind of natural piety that sustained him through periodic disillusionments. So the poems of *In What Hour* move agonizingly through historical struggles towards a transcendent view of humanity in and beyond perpetual cycles of nature.

The Phoenix and the Tortoise (1944)

Rexroth dedicated the short poems in the 1944 edition of *The Phoenix and the Tortoise* to D. H. Lawrence for attempting "to refound a spiritual family." Lawrence's "December Night"[2] is paraphrased in Rexroth's "Runaway" (*CSP*, 142); but whereas the English poet asks his lover to take off cloak, hat, and shoes by the fire, offering to warm her limbs with kisses, Rexroth goes much further, warming breasts and thighs also after describing his lover's damp hair, eyes, lips, and cold cheek, concluding with the wish to build a fire in her that would never go out, and to place a magnet in her that would always draw her home. Rexroth's poem sustains and develops desire that is more impulsive in Lawrence's poem.

Erotic mysticism pervades poems such as "Floating," in which time slips away in flesh (*CSP*, 144), and in "Inversely . . . ," in which the lovers are "implements " of lust (*CSP*, 148). But despair returns when the poet thinks of himself in "The Advantages of Learning" as ambitionless, friendless, poor, aging, and doomed (*CSP*, 146). Such despair is social as well as personal. The lost generation, Rexroth writes in "Between Two Wars," was not so lost as the oppressed masses (*CSP*, 150). And hearing "Madame Butterfly" on shortwave from London during World War II, he mourns the collapse of the civilization that he had taken for granted as a child before World War I ("Un Bel di Vendremo," *CSP*, 158). Bohemians who trivialize historical collapse disgust him (*CSP*, 147, 153, 166–67).

Nevertheless, love returns in a Christmas celebration (*CSP*, 143); in a commemoration of religious and political revolutionaries (*CSP*, 155); in the poem beginning "Climbing alone all day," in which Rexroth sensuously unites with his wife across the immense distance of a mountainside (*CSP*, 162–63); and most triumphantly and theologically in "Theory of Numbers," in which the bliss of Holy Matrimony focuses responsibility for all humankind (*CSP*, 164). The eroticism of these poems is grounded in Rexroth's organic philosophy. In the marvelously sensuous "We Come Back" (*CSP*, 163) and two excerpts reprinted from *The Homestead Called Damascus* (*CSP*, 159–60), for instance, erotic, seasonal, geological, and astronomical cycles triumph over accidents of existence.

Among satires, "Gas or Novacaine" (*CSP*, 151) denounces the impotence of intellectuals in the face of disaster, and "A Neoclassicist" (*CSP*, 167) ridicules a silly female mystic and priggish lecher. The mood changes in agonizing elegies to his mother, Delia (*CSP*, 153), and to Andrée (*CSP*, 154, 166), and in antiwar poems such as "Strength through Joy" (*CSP*, 156).

The completion of the long title poem (reprinted in *CLP*) is quietly celebrated in "Past and Future Turn About" (*CSP*, 168–72), in which the poet and Marie return in autumn to the Pacific beach where once again he contemplates dying sea creatures and geological records of millennia of life and death. He doubts all doctrines, including his own. Nor can the Cross be used as a weapon against injustice, for salvation comes only through selflessness. If anything lasts, it is cosmic patterns that change and disappear:

> Autumn comes
> And the death of flowers, but
> The flowered colored waves of
> The sea will last forever
> Like the pattern on the dress
> Of a beautiful woman.

Although in *The Phoenix and the Tortoise* there are terse satires (*CSP*, 153, 159, 166, 167) and tragic reminders of war (*CSP*, 156, 158, 161), Rexroth generally moves beyond despair into confident affections resting upon the order of nature, all expressed in consistently clear and direct language. The value of love is heightened by its brevity, by the transience of life itself. Ecstacy, celebrated both in present glory and poignant memory, gives meaning to loss. Rexroth has found his place in the universe, imagining with equanimity even his own death (*CSP*, 164).

The Signature of All Things (1950)

Rexroth borrowed the title of *The Signature of All Things* from Jacob Boehme, whose doctrine of correspondences is familiar to readers of Blake, Emerson, Whitman, and other romantics. "The whole outward visible world with all its being is a signature, or figure of the inward spiritual world," wrote Boehme,[3] whose most profound ecstacy occurred as he meditated on a dish reflecting the sunshine:[4] "In this light my spirit suddenly saw through all, and in all created things, even in herbs and grass, I knew God, who He is, how He is, and what His will is."[5] Rexroth alludes to this vision in "The Light on the Pewter Dish" (*CSP*, 209), and throughout this collection the light of love streams through the universe, most brilliantly in the title poem (actually a triple poem) in which, reading Boehme by a waterfall, he sees golden laurel leaves spinning down like the years of his life in a stream of love (*CSP*, 177). In a moonlit oak grove where black and white Holstein heifers lie under trees rooted in Indian graves, and in the startling correspondence between galaxies overhead and a phosphorescent log, there is no distinction between the spirit of the universe and what Rexroth sees, what he thinks, and what he says. Other signatures, in "Lyell's Hypothesis Again" (*CSP*, 180–81), for example, are marks on his wife's flesh that resemble marks of redwood cones in cliffs, and hardened lava which, like the ego, speaks of time.

Buddhism as well as Christian mysticism informs some of the poems in *The Signature of All Things*. In "Yugao" (*CSP*, 184), alluding to the glowing ghost of one of Prince Genji's lovers in the classic novel by Murasaki Shikibu, Rexroth imagines, as Marie sleeps peacefully, that an old jealousy from his own stormy life seeks karmic embodiment. "Hojiki," Japanese for "Monk's Record" or "Record of a Monk's Hut," alludes to a collection of poetic essays on Buddhist Emptiness by Kamono Chomei, written in 1212 A.D. In the center of Rexroth's sequence of seasonal nature poems with this title, preoccupied with wind, rain, waterfalls, and wildlife, he listens to the "speech" of falling water as he reads Christian saints in his mountain hut. Suddenly he remembers (*CSP*, 188):

> Buddha's infinite
> Laugh in the Lankavatara,
> Lighting up all the universes.
> The steep sides of the gorge enclose
> Me like the thighs of a girl's
> Body of bliss, and illusion, and law.

The Lankavatara is the sutra in which Shakyamuni bursts into laughter upon entering nirvana. Rexroth's simile of the mountain gorge as a girl's body is reminiscent of Lao-tzu's image of the Tao as a dark woman of the valley in the *Tao te Ching*; and in an ingenious Tantric twist, Rexroth identifies the girl's body with the triple body of the Buddha (Trikaya)—the three aspects of bliss (the experience of enlightenment, Sambhogakaya), illusion (the physical incarnation of Shakyamuni, Nirmanakaya), and law (or truth, Dharmakaya). On the last page of *The Signature of All Things* (*CSP*, 212), "Further Advantages of Learning" shows us the poet rummaging through a library, suddenly haunted by nirvana as he sees a photo of a vase of the Buddha's bones.

Rexroth's nirvanic consciousness of death also shapes some of his finest elegies for individuals and for humanity as a whole. In "Delia Rexroth," he reveres his mother as the muse of his early poems and paintings (*CSP*, 186). In a double poem for Andrée commemorating their love together in the mountains, he remembers great elegies by the Renaissance poet Henry King and the Chinese poet Yuan Chen, and Frieda Lawrence mourning as humankind moves towards oblivion (*CSP*, 190–92). In "Maximian, Elegy V," a woman tells him as they embrace in a redwood forest that she is weeping for the world (*CSP*, 195–96). Even when Buddhism is not explicitly mentioned, there is perennial compassion for universal suffering.

Four epistolary poems are for his friends Yvor Winters (*CSP*, 198–99), William Carlos Williams (*CSP*, 193–94), William Everson (Brother Antoninus, *CSP*, 201), and the Irish poet Kathleen Raine (*CSP*, 205–6); and other poems are for the actresses Geraldine Udell (*CSP*, 204) and Gardenia Chang (later to become Madam Mao, the leader of the Cultural Revolution in China, *CSP*, 199), García Lorca destroyed by fascism (*CSP*, 197) and a "Masseuse and Prostitute" (*CSP*, 179).

Among translations and imitations from Chinese, Greek, Latin, and Italian, the most stylistically and emotionally impressive, in its stately cadences, is "Leopardi—L'Infinito," in which shipwreck is sweet in the sea of infinity (*CSP*, 207). Clarity of vision, purity of language, directness of communication, a profound sense of peace and love, and a rich consistency of tone make this collection the most coherent and satisfying of all Rexroth's volumes of short poems.

The Dragon and the Unicorn (1952)

A few quiet and mellifluous excerpts from *The Dragon and the Unicorn* appear in *The Collected Shorter Poems*, although most of the long poem (reprinted in its entirety in *CLP*) is polemical, satirical, and dialectical. Two of these passages are from European travels: "Rosa Mundi" and "Golden Section"—lush, philosophical love lyrics set in the entanglements of history and myth, as sensuous as Rexroth's lover's body (*CSP*, 219).

The other six excerpts are from the last part of the long poem, when Rexroth returns to California, to Golden Gate Park, to rivers and canyons, and to the mountain cottage where he and Andrée were poor and happy two decades before (*CSP*, 222). In "Empty Mirror," he gazes into a campfire alone, remembering wars and adventures that he used to imagine in other fires, but now seeing only fire, free from the world of purpose (*CSP*, 223). This mystical equanimity is evident in placid imagery and lulling rhythms as, home again in nature, he sees at night spider-eyes shining in star-light reflected from his own eyes (*CSP*, 224).

In Defense of the Earth (1956)

Though sometimes associated with the Beat movement, which the poet soon criticised after welcoming it, *In Defense of the Earth* is no period piece, for these poems of timeless themes of love and protest, meditation and remembrance, stand out as some of his sturdiest. The original edition began with eight love poems for Marthe, but all references to her have been omitted in *The Collected Shorter Poems*, no doubt because of their divorce in 1948; and the seven poems for her have lost their original order and unity (*CSP*, 227–33, 243, 259). Nevertheless, they remain among his most affectionate poems, amplifying the erotic and matrimonial mysticism of *The Phoenix and the Tortoise* as he imagines his blood flowing out to the nebulas and back to him as light in which he sees Marthe's face. In this image cosmic and personal energies unite. Though sleeping, she communicates such deep love that he sees himself as a bird entangled in lies—a confession that intensifies to momentary speechlessness ("She is Away," *CSP*, 228–29). Haunted by the dead and by all impersonal forces he is sustained by erotic union. And in "The Great Canzon," a masterful translation of Dante, Rexroth identifies Marthe mystically with nature itself (*CSP*, 232):

> Time was, I saw
> Her dressed all in green, so lovely
> She would have made a stone love
> As I do, who love her very
> Shadow.

In the poems for their children called "The Lights in the Sky Are Stars," Rexroth imagines himself and others as "Vessels of the billion-year-long/River that flows now in your veins"—the cosmic "Bloodstream" (*CSP*, 237). These "vessels" are, I think, not only blood vessels, channels of the universal energy-stream, but can be seen also as ships in the cosmic river, or even utensils such as bowls holding spirit. Contemplating the heavenly bodies, he no longer knows where he begins and ends, for his eye is the universe seeing itself (*CSP*, 238). The periodicity of Halley's Comet and other heavenly cycles harmonize memories of his childhood with his children's present and future, if they can escape from being destroyed by depersonalizing men and their bloody ideas (*CSP*, 238, 241). His daughter asks whether the blood on the moon, during an eclipse, is because of all the blood on earth (*CSP*, 243). Against the inhumanity of civilization, he offers a primitve religion of the moon, humanity, Christmas, Easter, and birthdays (*CSP*, 242–43).

Among poems about Rexroth's youth, "The Bad Old Days" recalls the revolutionary vow that he made at age thirteen, horrified by wasted faces of the poor in the Chicago stock yards (*CSP*, 258–59). And "A Living Pearl" tells about his first trip west, at age sixteen, riding freights and training wild horses. The title is taken from Dante's image of moonlight, as he recalls how the western landscape first opened his mind to organic forms (*CSP*, 235–37). And while mountain-climbing in "Time Is the Mercy of Eternity," one of his richest visionary poems, he becomes clear as crystal (*CSP*, 251).

But love of nature never seduces him from the passion of liberating humanity from injustices. Commemorating an old comrade who dies after realizing that their utopian dreams would not come true for a very long time, if ever, "For Eli Jacobson" glorifies revolutionary struggles between the World Wars that made them happy with hope (*CSP*, 244–45). And in a group of nature poems for his daughter Mary, the beauties of nature are contrasted with the threat of war (*CSP*, 260–65).

"Thou Shalt Not Kill," Rexroth's most famous protest poem which he recorded with jazz accompaniment, denounces cold-war enemies of mankind, established elites on both sides of the iron curtain who destroy the genius of youth. This "Memorial for Dylan Thomas" is a public sacrament of mourning and righteous outrage. Commemorating dozens of poets who went mad or died violently in acquisitive, competitive, predatory, warring societies, both capitalistic and communistic, he echoes "Lament for the Makeris" by Scottish poet William Dunbar:

> What happened to Robinson,
> Who used to stagger down Eighth Street,
> Dizzy with solitary gin?
> Where is Masters, who crouched in
> His law office for ruinous decades?

> Where is Leonard who thought he was
> A locomotive? and Lindsay,
> Wise as a dove, innocent
> As a serpent, where is he?
> Timor mortis conturbat me[6]

Demanding to know who killed Dylan Thomas, "The bird of Rhiannon" (*CSP*, 272), he attacks celebrities who have created a culture of death: Oppenheimer, Einstein, Hemingway, Eliot. The assumption of total moral liability in the longer poems would suggest that much of Rexroth's indignation explodes from his own necessary involvement in the very culture that he despises. Though self-righteous and at times unfair, he has unforgettably subverted the "social lie" that has destroyed dozens of poets and other creative youth. "Thou Shalt Not Kill" is Rexroth's greatest protest poem because of its eloquently expressed range of feeling from tender sympathy to bewilderment, then to prophetic rage and accusatory assault, all grounded in brutalities of history.[7]

"A Bestiary" is a proverbial sequence for Rexroth's daughters, warning them against conformity, cuteness, power, money, parasitism, the state, fakery, myths, authorities, and epigrammatically initiating them into some fundamental truths, such as, "N is for nothing. There is/Much more of it than something" (*CSP*, 280). Another satirical series for his daughters, "Mother Goose," contains his most whimsical poems (*CSP*, 285–92).

After miscellaneous epigrams, diatribes, and translations comes a finale of three poems on the philosophical nature of poetry. The first poem in a pair called "They Say This Isn't a Poem" ironically sums up the theory of Leibniz's preestablished harmony, which had once attracted Rexroth, but which turns out to stink of oppression and violence (*CSP*, 312). The second poem of this pair presents Rexroth's, and Homer's, alternate view that Nature's apparent order is only a reflection "Of the courage, loyalty,/Love, and honesty of men" (*CSP*, 313). Finally, "Codicil" tells us that the theory of poetry as impersonal construction as applied by Eliot, Valery, Pope, and others generates just its opposite, intimate revery (*CSP*, 314). These three poems succinctly reveal contradictory concerns that Rexroth struggled throughout his life to reconcile in his poetry: his intuitions of a transcendent metaphysical harmony on the one hand, and immanent personalism on the other; or put another way, the amorality of existence and the demand for justice.

Here then is a reaffirmation of the person, even when masked in so-called impersonal art, a fitting finale for a volume in which Rexroth comes through so robustly as lover, father, and prophet denouncing the injustices of humanity while at the same time recognizing its place in the creative process of nature.

Natural Numbers (1963)

The Collected Shorter Poems concludes with "New Poems," written between 1957 and 1962, from the original 1963 edition of *Natural Numbers*, which had also included selections from the previous books. Notably missing are poems of intricate philosophizing and of extreme technical innovation, although a gentle cubism is apparent in "Eight for Ornette's Music" (*CSP*, 332–34). Nearly all of the other "New Poems" are in the more natural direct statement in syllabics, and the prevailing tone is elegiac instead of lyrical or satirical.

In many of them the poet is hiking or fishing with his daughters; listening to Mary , at seven, talk about "Homer in Basic" (*CSP*, 317); reminiscing about the time of revolutionary optimism ("Fish Peddler and Cobbler," another of his perennial memorials for Sacco and Vanzetti, *CSP*, 319); or remembering his father flipping poker chips that three-year-old Katherine now plays with. A dozen poems of traveling in France, Italy, and England resemble passages in *The Dragon and the Unicorn*, but we find none of the harshness of the earlier satires, for he has moved from polemics to tragic acceptance of the human condition.

The book ends with a sequence called "Air and Angels," love poems with the insistent, sad reminder of inevitable loss and loneliness, as in Matthew Arnold's "Dover Beach," which Rexroth quotes in "Pacific Beach" (*CSP*, 340–41). Nothing can save him from the overriding sense of doom surrounding moments of ecstacy. The quieter, resigned, more traditional side of his personality emerges as he consolidates his lifework to date in a mood of solitary tenderness. He explores such perennial themes as children, youth, love, and community with elegiac equanimity, which in five years would be enriched by the pervasive influence of his first visit to Japan. The cool lyricism of the poems written for music, at the conclusion of *The*

Collected Shorter Poems, harmonizes in style and tone with some of the poems in "Gödel's Proof" at its beginning: so the whole collection is cyclic, like nature itself.

And like nature, multiple rhythms unite Rexroth's poetry from beginning to end. His pioneering preoccupation with elemental sounds of language, most evident in cubist poems that allied him, for a time, with Zukofsky's experiments in verbal musicality, extends throughout *The Collected Shorter Poems*, so lyrics in "natural numbers" also display amazingly subtle rhythmic and melodic qualities inherent in the duration, pitch, and stress of common speech. Alternations of concrete and abstract diction, passages of pure vision that resolve philosophical dialectics, are also rhythmic, as are dramatic variations in tone from despair, agony, and indignation to desire, affection, and ecstacy. The selection, arrangement, and meaning of some poems, especially in the cubist mode, may trouble readers, but there are more significant, interrelated patterns of sound, syntax, imagery, tone, and theme, and more enduring wisdom, than most readers can discover in a lifetime of close reading. *The Collected Shorter Poems* is a work of heroic struggle, artistic and intellectual, that deserves as much attention as the work of any modern poet.

The Collected Longer Poems (1968)

Rexroth thought of his long philosophical reveries in a tradition that included Aiken's *Symphonies*, Eliot's *The Waste Land*, Pound's *The Cantos*, Williams's *Paterson*, Zukofsky's *Poem Beginning "A"*, Lowenfels's *Some Deaths*, and Tyler's *Granite Butterfly*.[8] He might have added Whitman's *Leaves of Grass*, and outside American literature the prophetic poetry of Blake, Milton, Dante, Lao-tzu, and the Bible. But his claim in the introduction to *The Collected Longer Poems* (1968) that the five poems are one poem does not quite ring true, for the five are too stylistically diverse to be considered unified. Moreover, the long delays before the first two poems were published in books, more than three decades for *Homestead* and two decades for *Prolegomenon*, indicate lingering artistic and intellectual uncertainties about his youthful symbolist and cubist innovations. Nevertheless, the three later long poems are major achievements, and the five considered together impressively reveal the development of the poet's artistry, worldview, and wisdom. Of these, *The Phoenix and the Tortoise* and *The Dragon and the Unicorn* expand the radical Christian personalism of the first two poems, whereas *The Heart's Garden, The Garden's Heart* initiates the predominantly Buddhist outlook of the last thirteen years of his life, although oriental influences had affected his work from its inception.

Rexroth explains in the introduction that the plot of the five poems is "the interior and exterior adventures of two poles of a personality," represented in *Homestead* by two brothers (with a third figure, an anonymous observer-narrator commenting from time to time). In dialogue, philosophies are contradicted dialectically and resolved only in a transcendent experience. Male personae in the poems and plays—the brothers in *Homestead*, Rexroth himself undisguised in the other poems, and Greek heroes in *Beyond the Mountains*—form a polarity with fertility figures such as the Greek Artemis, Marichi (an Indian Goddess of the Dawn), and human heroines who suggest an absolute community of love realized in "the self unselfing itself" in "creative process."

The Homestead Called Damascus (1957): 1920–1925

The title of Rexroth's first long philosophical reverie reminds us of St. Paul's conversion, and *The Homestead Called Damascus* is rich in Christian imagery and the kind of religious anthropology that Eliot, Frazer, and Cambridge classicists had been promoting. Is the homestead domestic or monastic? And are the heroes blood-brothers or religious brothers? Thomas is associated with Doubting Thomas Didymus and the sacrificed god Tammus-Osiris-Adonis-Dionysus, expressing the involuntary, reflective side of Rexroth's personality. Sebastian, paradoxically identified with the Greek god Eros as well as with the saint shot with arrows, reflects the active, willful side of the poet, who finally gravitates from action to contemplation of the fertility-goddess-muses Marichi and a Negro blues singer. Sebastian also compares himself in one of Rexroth's earliest oriental allusions to Daruma (*CLP*, 12), the Japanese name of Bodhidharma, the monk who brought Zen Buddhism from India to China, meditating so long that his legs rotted away.

Homestead is in four parts, in Rexroth's most musical, symbolist style, in lines typically of nine syllables. He begins by contrasting angels who never question the mysteries of the universe with youths who search infinity for spiritual vocations as they construct forms to make sense of their chaotic lives. The brothers live on the Hudson River in the Catskills, in a rambling homestead that embodies the bourgeois-Christian-classical tradition from which they try in vain to escape. Their parents might have been created by Henry James or Proust, and their grandfather had stuffed the house with reminders of imperialistic glories in India and China; while under the church are pterodactyl bones and smoky paintings of libidinous primitivism repressed by civilization and superego. In a neighboring mansion of bygone Renaissance glory, the brothers visit Leslie, who lives like a princess.

Unsettled by artifice, domesticity, and decadence, the brothers contemplate heroic quests and ancient fertility rites, the origins of culture; but fearful of losing themselves in either sexual love or martyrdom, they never find the grace that came to Saul on the road to Damascus, to pagans in search of Atlantis, or to knights in quest of the Holy Grail. They kid each other with myths, but the serious reveries of Sebastian waver between enticements of domestic bliss with Leslie and, at the other extreme, the martyrdom that befell his Christian namesake of the third century. Thomas has nihilistic night-mares of Lucifer and Modred (the nephew and murderer of King Arthur) who could see only the potters' field, though Christ was always present.

In Part II, "The Autumn of Many Years," while Thomas goes on an erotic quest to New York City, Sebastian sinks into a tempo-rary nirvana, but leaves it to ponder the wasteland of the city and Maxine, the black stripper and earth goddess whose promises he cannot experience. Suddenly, the narrator breaks in like Eliot's Tiresias, ranting of mad lotus-eaters, Adonis castrated, and evolu-tionary mysteries of creative process, geological, biological, astro-nomical, and human (*CLP*, 13–14). This remarkable vision, informed by scientific knowledge spurned by Eliot, is followed by a scene of the debased union of Persephone and Adonis reminiscent of Eliot's "The Game of Chess" (*CLP*, 14–15). Part II ends on Good Friday as the brothers sink into contemplation, but without receiv-ing grace.

In Part III, "The Double Hellas" (Apollonian and Dionysian) the universe is perceived in aesthetic forms: "Baroque forests," Bach's bust in a park, "sculpt and colored stones and shells" (*CLP*, 20, 17, 23, 29). The brothers are still paralyzed in the dilemma between the promise of decadent domesticity with Leslie in a ménage à trois, and the dangers of sacrifice involving such fertility goddesses as Persephone, Kore, Theano, and the living Maxine. While the brothers fantasize, the narrator seems to be caressing an actual woman (*CLP*, 25).

In the last part, "The Stigmata of Fact," during an archaeological expedition that is a kind of grail quest, Thomas concludes (*CLP*, 13) that

> "There is no self subsistent
> Microcosm." He thinks a while of
> Chuang Tzu fishing with a straight pin and
> Says, "There is no self subsistent
> Macrocosm either."

Here Thomas is echoing Shakyamuni who, under the Bo tree, discovered that there is no absolute universal spirit (Brahman) and no absolute personal self (Atman): experiencing universal interdependence, he gave up striving for any absolute, finding nirvana in change itself. Chuang Tzu, the Chinese sage popular in Taoism and Zen, was so completely, unselfconsciously attuned to nature that he needed no fishhook. Sebastian agrees with his brother, quoting Shakyamuni that "There is no self that suffers release," but without attaining enlightenment (*CLP*, 35); nor can Maxine's enticements save him from sterility. Silence closes about Thomas, resignedly staring into a fire.

Any reading of this astonishing poem discerns only some of the many threads of meaning woven into the ambiguities of its symbolism and ideas, making it as philosophically intricate as Eliot's or Stevens's poetry. The Damascan brothers are adolescent Prufrocks, inhibited from making a leap of faith into love or matrydom, but are more sensuous, humorous, and intellectual than Eliot's antihero. No poem is more faithful to the frustrations and speculations of precocious youth. The brothers are not dramatically distinct, nor do they act in a definitive way, but symbolist personae are not accustomed to do so. Unlike most symbolist literature, *Homestead* contains abundant diction from mathematics and the natural sciences—"galaxy, dark nebulae," "space—Euclidean, warped, or otherwise," "rhomboids, nonagons" (*CLP*, 3), and technical terms from geology and the life sciences intertwining with mythological language. Here we see the beginnings of Rexroth's organic philosophy, uniting mystical experience with scientific observation and theory, which led to a more direct and ecstatic contemplation of nature in later poems. And the erotic mysteries that are pursued in *Homestead* are later realized in many lyrics.

"A Prolegomenenon to a Theodicy" (1932): 1925–1927

How can God be omniscient, omnipotent, and supremely good if evil exists? A theodicy, such as Leibniz's theory of pre-established harmony, justifies God's perfection in relation to an imperfect universe. Rexroth did not offer a solution to this problem, but his second long poem concerns mystical experience without which no theodicy is possible. Religiously and technically more mature than *Homestead*, "A Prolegomenon to a Theodicy" is his most famous cubist work, placing him securely in the international arena of the Revolution of the Word.

Metaphysical and moral despair is much harsher in this poem than in *Homestead*, in which the Damascan brothers had the luxury of witty dialogue, congenial sentiments, and sensuous companions. In Part I of "Prolegomenon," communication seems hopeless as the distraught poet speaks in extreme dissociation to a disembodied "you" who seems not to understand him.

Part II suggests various ways of existing, in short, parallel lines like those of a primitive chant, a style sustained and intensified in Parts III and IV, which ends with revelations of lamp and mirror.[9] In Part V, voices praise the Lord in a hymn of peace. In Part VI the poet is compared to a blissful Thomist angel who contemplates the Word and all things in it. In Part VII the poet is tempted to evade his prophetic responsibilities, but in Part VIII he is reminded that moral character requires the choice of death rather than dishonor. In Part IX he imagines a Dantean hell.

In these depths of misery, the poet hears from the sky that it is blessed to die; and a visitor, apparently a Savior, is admitted by the woman to whom the poet had addressed the opening part of the poem. In the last part, the poet moves climactically towards a kind of "Paradise Regained." First, he is assured by Aristotle that he will reach his goal and then by Blake's greater wisdom that "Aristotle was but the rubbish of an Adam" (*CLP*, 58). The angel Gabriel defeats the evil spirit and the poet is blessed by the coming of God in Apocalypse (*CLP*, 60):

> The ciborium of the abyss
> The bread of light
> The chalice of the byss
> The wine of flaming light
> The wheeling multitude
> The rocking cry

In "Prolegomenon" Rexroth reaches out of the despair of *Homestead* towards God Himself. But the Beatific Vision, bursting through the radical dissociation of the rest of the poem, strains belief, and nothing so blatant appears again in his work. The fact that the work was not published in a book-length collection of his poems until 1949, more than two decades after it had been written, may indicate serious uncertainty about its outlook and effectiveness. Although certain passages in it are powerful, it is the least satisfying of the long reveries. Nevertheless, its prosody is extraordinary: for instance (*CLP*, 46–47):

> The throat of night
> The plethora of wine
> The fractured hour of light
> The opaque lens
> The climbing wheel

Here the patterns of sound are subtly woven: *t*'s in *throat, night, light* (and rhyme also); *i*'s in *night, wine, light, climbing*; *l*'s in *plethora, light, lens, wheel*; and reverberations in *throat* and *plethora*. Also the cubism of this poem produces cadences closer to those of actual speech than the symbolist mellifluences of *Homestead*; and the Damascan brothers seem dilletantish in contrast to the rigorous asceticism of the poet in "Prolegomenon." It prepared the way for Rexroth's first book eight years later.

The Phoenix and the Tortoise (1944): 1940–1944

In the sacramental union of lovers Rexroth found a solution to the problem of the one and the many in both moral and metaphysical terms. His third long poem and his first extended masterpiece, *The Phoenix and the Tortoise*, like "The Phoenix and the Turtle," the mystical poem attributed to Shakespeare, celebrates the erotic union of opposites. It also reveals a process from despair through erotic and matrimonial mysticism to a consciousness of universal responsibility.

Rexroth's despair had festered from the loss of his parents during World War I, the collapse of a humane way of life that he had taken for granted as a child, the disillusionment of growing up in a predatory society, the execution of Sacco and Vanzetti in 1927, the rise of fascism, the depression, the Moscow Trials, the Spanish Civil War, and the death of Andrée in 1940, at the outset of World War II. Ecstatic experiences from time to time, however, had reaffirmed his intuition that the universe is, after all, harmonious in some inexplicable way, an intuition that seemed to be confirmed by mystical writings that influenced his own. The personalism, sacramentalism, and sense of reponsibility in *The Phoenix and the Tortoise* clearly come from Christianity, but Buddhism is also, less obviously, a major source, shaping this poem far more than it had affected *Homestead* and foreshadowing the preponderantly Buddhist outlook of later work.

The true person, he argues, is not an isolated self, but a lover in harmony with the universe. The idea, developed throughout the poem, is familiar in Christianity; and though compassion is emphasized more than love in Buddhism, the Bodhisattva, like Christ, is a sacrificial savior. Shakyamuni's idea of no-self appears in Rexroth's allusion, for example, to a waka by the Japanese poet Kintsune: "The flowers whirl away in the wind like snow. / The thing that falls away is myself."[10]

Rexroth acknowledged the central influence on *The Phoenix and the Tortoise* of *The Flower Wreath Sutra* (Sanskrit *Avatamsaka* or Japanese *Kegon*), after which one of his last poems is entitled.[11] The ideas of this sutra were said to be so obscure to Shakyamuni's followers that he soon gave up preaching them, relying instead on the elementary Four Noble Truths (on the cause and ending of suffering), the Eight Fold Path, and Interdependent Origination.[12] In this sutra, the ultimate reality of creation and destruction is revealed in a grain of dust or anything else, just as William Blake saw "the world in a grain of sand."[13] According to Kūkai (Kōbō Daishi, Rexroth's favorite theorist of Japanese Buddhism), the Buddha in this sutra preached that each moment is infinite, that particulars are universal, and that everything is infinitely interdependent, using images of lamps and Indra's Net.[14] Over the castle of the god Indra hangs an immense net in which countless jewels at the intersections reflect one another as well as the whole, just as mirrors placed around lamps reflect them endlessly, and just as everything in the universe reflects everything else and the whole: so each impermanent, insubstantial thing in the phenomenal world (samsara) reflects the transcendent realm (nirvana) and is inseparable from it: form is void and void is form.

This theme of universal interaction permeates *The Phoenix and the Tortoise*, extending the organic philosophy that Rexroth had been developing for two decades. In fact, Buddhism complemented Leibnitz's philosophy of preestablished harmony that had strongly influenced Rexroth's organicism.[15] Rejecting the alienating, destructive pressures of modern secular thought and history, in which each person is reduced to an atomic individual in perpetual conflict with other individuals, the poet comes to realize, like a Bodhisattva, his ecological interdependence with all beings, and his ethical responsibility for all persons, including each war victim. He is not a lone individual, but participates in all nature and history, wherever he is, nourished by the entire universe and changing it with his every act.

Indra's net is behind such images as webs of misery and accident that unite the poet with all suffering beings, such as the drowned Japanese sailor lying among other dead creatures on the Pacific shore, at the outset of the poem (*CLP*, 63–65, 85). Contemplating geological strata and reading Plutarch, Rexroth wonders what survives from the waste of history, concluding that modern civilization is disintegrating in war just as classical civilization did. Is there a way out? Like Socrates, he doubts each answer that occurs to him. At one point in his speculations he seems to agree with Aristotle that "Poetry is more philosophic than history," but always breaks out of the circle of argumentation (*CLP*, 65, 67, 68, 70). Condemning theories of personality and history in which reason, ego, and will are basic, he discovers the transcendent person in preparing Passover supper on Easter Eve (*CLP*, 66), after which he and his wife Marthe make love. In half-sleep, he has a vision, inspired by Jacob Boehme, of the universe as an hour glass in which gold and silver sands fall and rise from God (*CLP*, 72). Christian and Buddhist images mix as Easter approaches (*CLP*, 72–73):

The moonlight of the Resurrection,
The moon of Amida on the sea,
Glitters on the wings of the bombers,
Illuminates the darkened cities.
. . . .
    Amida,
Kwannon, turn from peace. As moonlight
Flows on the tides, innumerable
Dark worlds flow into splendor.

Here the full moon is the image of Dharmakaya (the Body of Buddhist Truth) in *The Flower Wreath Sutra*. Amida (the Japanese name for Amitabha in Sanskrit) means Infinite Light and is the name of the Buddha of the Western Paradise or Pure Land, the incarnation of Compassion. Kwannon (or Kannon, Japanese for Avalokiteshvara in Sanskrit) is the Bodhisattva of Compassion. These beings turn from the peace of their own enlightenment to save all suffering beings.

In PartII Rexroth is indignantly anarchistic in the tradition of Piotr Kropotkin, Mikhail Bakunin, and the Industrial Workers of the World: "The State is the organization/Of the evil instincts of mankind." And: "War is the health of the State? Indeed!/War is the State" (*CLP*, 74–75). Extreme shifts of style from exploding epigrams to sensuous imagery, from ferocious rhetoric to somber elegy, cohere in the person of the poet in the poem, a passionate thinker and contemplative actor. Nearing sleep in frosty moonlight, he remembers heroes, martyrs, and poets such as Nicias, More, and Abelard who transcend the waste of history (*CLP*, 78).

Waking beside his wife at dawn, in Part III, Rexroth rages again against the impersonality of history (*CLP*, 80–81), in which I-It supplants Buber's I-Thou. Berating intellectuals who sell themselves to the state, he ironically contrasts the Sophist Hippias, with the most salable skills, contending with the wiser Socrates, who sells nothing (*CLP*, 82–83). But why think at all? Dreams may be as true as reason (*CLP*, 85).

Finally, in Part IV, the rising sun of Good Friday reminds Rexroth of the purity of the universe (*CLP*, 87), an idea from the *Flower Wreath Sutra*, in which the sun of Intelligence or Dharmakaya rises on all indiscriminately, though some beings are in the dark longer than others, just as plains lie longer in shadow than do peaks. Buddhist and Christian themes fuse in the finale as the poet meditates on Schweitzer, to whom the poem is dedicated, and other saintly persons. Remembering a miraculous rainbow and crosses in the sky reported by Whymper, the Matterhorn explorer, Rexroth feels the rising sun focus through him to inifinity (*CLP*, 91):

> Men drop dead in the ancient rubbish
> Of the Acropolis, scholars fall
> Into self-dug graves, Jews are smashed
> Like heroic vermin in the Polish winter.
> This is my fault, the horrible term
> Of weakness, evasion, indulgence,
> The total of my petty fault—
> No other man's.

In a powerful affirmation of love and sacramental marriage in which enlightenment comes erotically, Rexroth celebrates his wife as a focus of the whole universe. As she comes towards him through the breakers, nude and singing, the sun illuminates her, the moon, and the sea, melting ancient ice (*CLP*, 91).

The Phoenix and the Tortoise, a glorious contribution to mystical literature, unites personal experience with the tragedy of history and the ever-renewing interactivities of nature. Oriental wisdom renews and expands the familiar Christian message of selfless love. Rexroth's reply to war, and to human misery generally, rises from an acute philosophical and spiritual struggle and culminates in matrimonial bliss that sacramentalizes a profound vision of the universe. The style ranges from lyrical sensuousness to abstract argument, and from an elegiac sense of the tragedy of history to ecstatic symbolism, rich in Japanese lore and allusions, all sounding from a distinct and compelling voice.[16]

The Dragon and the Unicorn (1952)

Rexroth compared the tone of *The Dragon and the Unicorn*, his longest poem, to that of Mark Twain's travel writings[17]; but in Rexroth's poem, along with satirical passages reminiscent of *Innocents Abroad*, there is more abstruse philosophizing about the political and religious complexities of European history, focused on the meaning of love, than Twain would find palatable. Rexroth's personality has grown more complex in this, his fourth long revery, than in his earlier work. In the later poem are particularized responses to the cold war and atomic terror in Europe and America as well as a comprehensive development of the worldview delineated in *The Phoenix and the Tortoise*, which it closely resembles also in the natural style of direct statement. The idea of community, hitherto expressed abstractly for the most part, is concretized in *The Dragon and the Unicorn* in encounters with friends in Europe trying to recover from two world wars and under the threat of a third. Rexroth is more active, and interactive, in this poem than in any other of his entire career. Returning to California mountains, he reenters the wilderness to contemplate organic forms as raccoons stare at him from a campfire. Man of nature, sophisticated traveler, dialectical philosopher, anarchistic polemicist, and visionary lover are fused in the person intimately speaking to us.

The poem begins with the question of love, asked by Pilate as he washes his hands. In Part I, as Rexroth crosses America by train from San Francisco to New York, and then tours England, part of it by foot—Liverpool, Wales, Shropshire, Tintern Abbey, Bath, Somerset, Stonehenge, London—he searches for the answer that would bring spiritual renewal to a world wrecked by two world wars and preparing for another. Pilate's amorality characterizes those who rule the world, denying the creative power of interpersonal love. Recalling the Buddha's Fire Sermon (*CLP*, 95), Rexroth suggests that the way out of world catastrophe is an erotic path of enlightenment familiar in Tantra, though it was considered heretical by other Buddhists. He lists seductive women linked with Shakyamuni (*CLP*, 98); he suggests the union of the Buddha's compassion and Tara's wisdom in a traditional image derived from Tantric mandala of *yabyum*, or sexual yoga (*CLP*, 214–15); and he lists additional male/female polarities in major world religions: Kali and Shiva, Artemis and Apollo, the Shekinah and Jehovah, Mary and God, Magdalene and Christ (*CLP*, 274).

From nirvana of enlightened union, to samsara, illusory experience that is usually taken for granted as the "real" world, Rexroth's attention swings back and forth. Vacant lots in Chicago remind him of Andrew Marvell's deserts of eternity (*CLP*, 97), and when he tours England, bombed-out shells of Liverpool remind him of the fall of Rome (*CLP*, 100). Poverty, war, the collapse of civilization are consequences of the amoral use of human beings as means to an abstract, impersonal end. They are not respected as persons but are instead made to serve history under the illusion that time is abstractly objective, linear and atomic, rather than an organic dimension of human experience. When time is made to dominate life, extreme dehumanization is represented by the logical positivist, who rejects the truth of any experience that cannot be scientifically verified and who denies the wholeness of organic process by categorically separating fact from value. Modern science, technology, and politics conspire to quantify persons.

Against this worldview, Rexroth's basis for renewal is the sense of reality as communion among persons. The image of Indra's Net from *The Flower Wreath Sutra*, introduced in *The Phoenix and the Tortoise*, generates this remarkably intricate conception of universal interpersonal mutuality (*CLP*, 108):

> Each moment of the universe
> And all the universes
> Are reflected in each other
> And in all their parts and
> Thence again in themselves
> As a concourse of persons, all
> Reflecting and self-reflecting
> And the reflections and the
> Reflective medium reflecting.

So the self or ego, as the Buddha taught, does not exist in itself but is only a perspective on other perspectives; and the person, inseparable from the creative process itself, is responsible for the universe (*CLP*, 112–13). Rexroth had arrived at this conclusion in *The Phoenix and the Tortoise*, but here the idea is ontological: being is ethical. Reality is responsibility because a person is the universe he or she creates: or in terms of Vedanta, Atman is Brahman, Thou Art That! The Universal responsibility inherent in mutuality implies that all creatures have Buddha-mind (*CLP*, 118). Love turns out to be the act of creation and evaluation itself (*CLP*, 121), exemplified as this poem, a reply to Pilate's cynicism.

In Part II, the poet feels an immense ethical burden from the waste of human exploitation. Hearing the popular song "La Vie en Rose" again and again as he travels through France, he suffers memories of failed or broken love (*CLP*, 123–24); and along with the pain of his own loss, he feels the agony of history as he recalls the Inquisition as well as the recent war (*CLP*, 141). Wherever he goes, he is reminded of repression and waste. How can a man of conscience endure? Must he empathize with each individual sufferer as a Bodhisattva renounces Buddhahood for himself in order to help humanity find enlightenment? In lieu of this extreme commitment, Rexroth's alternative is to seek transcendence through the contemplative practice of erotic love, which sacramentally universalizes the person (*CLP*, 154).

In Part III, as if in fulfillment of this idea of love, his third wife, Marthe, conceives a child as they tour Italy together. As in previous sections, philosophizing is interspersed with anecdotal passages satirical of depersonalizing forces such as American capitalism, leftist intellectuals, the Vatican, and all states (*CLP*, 207). As the poet talks with wealthy intellectuals and poor workers, epigrams become more compressed. Love is defined as "mutual indwelling/Without grasping" (*CLP*, 158): "A Person is a lover" (*CLP*, 160). He denounces the perversions of modern marriage, based upon commodities (*CLP*, 167–68), and the antisexual repressiveness of the Catholic hierarchy (*CLP*, 182). The orgiastic communion of Tantric and ancient Hebrew religions was based upon a community of lovers, which is Rexroth's idea of God (*CLP*, 170–75). And when he asserts that all experience is that of a "Contemplative immersed in/Contemplation," he suggests that each person is intrinsically though unknowingly a Buddha (*CLP*, 176).

Community is always threatened by "collectivity," reducing persons to numbers as the state and prevailing economic systems, both capitalistic and communistic, do. In a world of political and military regimentation, technological coercion, and war, true love is subversive, cultish, in perpetual opposition to the dehumanizing illusion of collectivity (*CLP*, 191). Believing in the lie of the state, people allow themselves to be coerced, depersonalized, and destroyed. The only alternative to despair is to love, conscious of the love of others (*CLP*, 222).

In Part IV, while passing through Switzerland, Rexroth denounces the obscurantism of Karl Barth's theology and Jung's psychotherapy (*CLP*, 226); and in Paris, reflecting on failed revolutions as communities destroyed by collectivities, he rejects the

Marxist idea that the proletariat as a collectivity can usher in the good society (*CLP*, 230–32). He finds radical workers of sensibility and talent who are not, however, about to sacrifice themselves at the barricades for remote, impersonal objectives (*CLP*, 236–41). Their ideology is less important than their respect and affection for one another.

In the final section, back in America, traveling alone from the east coast to California, he stops in Chicago and Kansas City long enough to look up a couple of girl friends and to rail at the Protestant ethic (*CLP*, 253). Out west, beyond civilization founded upon the denial of love, his thoughts travel "beyond the mountains" as he sits peacefully in a mountain cottage where he and his first wife had been poor and happy artists, lovers, contemplatives (*CLP*, 265).

The Dragon and the Unicorn is a major effort to work out a coherent worldview, an original fusion of insights from major religions, but concludes like all of Rexroth's long poems in visionary experience beyond abstract speculation. The sustained interior monologue, which often becomes critical dialogue as every idea is vigorously tested, reveals an uncompromisingly conscientious person who lets nothing unexamined slip past. Debating other intellectuals or making love to women in bombed out slums of Europe or in unspoiled mountains of California, he articulates the universal in the particular, the mutuality of existence in each observation. Christian themes of communion, moral responsibility, holy matrimony, and the universal community of love are realized more fully than in any of his other poems. In the context of the creative process of nature, imagined through Buddhist imagery, transcendence is experienced in immanence, and immanence is transcendent. He has expanded his mastery of thought and language, here, generally, in seven to nine syllable lines, even beyond the accomplishments of his preceding poems. Epigrammatical, rhetorical, and philosophical passages are as memorable as sensuously lyrical and elegiac lines.

Having fulfilled his aims in writing this kind of dialectical poem, he abandoned the western mode of philosophical debate in his next long revery, *The Heart's Garden, The Garden's Heart*, producing his most sustained expression of pure visionary experience.

The Heart's Garden, The Garden's Heart (1967)

In Rexroth's fifth and last long philosophical poem, the aging poet wanders through Japanese forests at the beginning of summer, recalling Lao-tzu's imagery of the Tao: "The valley's soul is death-less./It is called the dark woman./The dark woman is the gate/To the root of heaven and earth" (*CLP*, 283). He feels towards the Tao like a man who has lost the woman he loves. But since illumination is like the innocence of fish who do not know that they live in water, the desire for it is self-defeating. The Tao is like light, but unseen, and like music, but unheard. He loses himself in intermingling sensa-tions of bamboo leaves, gold fish, waterfalls, birds, birdlike voices of women, temple bells, meadows, lakes, the perfume of flowers and forests (*CLP*, 283–86). The Tao, the radiant harmony of life, both immanent and transcendent, speaks in his pulse and breathing (*CLP*, 290). Wandering over mountains and through valleys bathed with light, conversing with tree frogs, hearing the click of looms and the clack of pachinko machines, he experiences things as they are, freed from illusions born of grasping (*CLP*, 297). To the enlightened eye, nothing is specially "holy" in opposition to the "profane": so an ordinary stone or uncarved block of wood is no less sacred than a temple. Similarly, any human act, even the prostitute's, is con-templative (*CLP*, 299).

The language of this poem is as sensuous as the perceptions that it conveys. No other poem of Rexroth's is more musical. Rather than theorizing, he transmits experience directly through such melodious imagery as:

> The Eve of Ch'ing Ming—Clear Bright,
> A quail's breast sky and smoky hills,
> The great bronze gong booms in the
> Russet sunset. Late tonight
> It will rain. Tomorrow will
> Be clear and cool once more. One more
> Clear, bright day in this floating life.

How simple the sense, but how intricate the sounds of this passage (*CLP*, 294). The first five lines, like most of the others in the poem, are of seven syllables each; but the five stresses in each of the first two lines make them seem languidly long in contrast to the abruptness of the third and fourth. The indecisive ending of the third line and, in the fourth, the internal rhyme ("Russet sunset"), the caesura, and the *s*'s and *t*'s, contribute to the change of pace; and the sixth and seventh lines are a return to the languor of the "floating life" of detached equanimity.

Patterns of vowels and consonants also give the passage contour. First there are three stressed *ee*'s and internal rhyme: "The Eve of Ch'ing Ming." "Clear Bright," the name of the day which describes the day, is repeated in the last line, and "clear" is also in the sixth. "Breast," "bronze," and "booms" alliterate with "Bright"; "tonight" rhymes with it; and the *i*'s in "sky" and "life" provide additional linkage. Playing against the *i*'s are the low resonance of the *o*'s and *u*'s in "smoke," "bronze gong booms," "Russet sunset," "tonight" and "Tomorrow," "cool once more. One more," and "floating." The *t*'s of "Bright," "breast," "great," "Russet sunset. Late tonight," "tomorrow," and, repeated in the last line, "bright," lead to "floating"; and *f* and *l* reappear in "life." The poem must be read aloud for the reader to enter fully this "floating life."

Just as everyday objects are sacred to the enlightened eye, so the most ordinary words become music conveying the feeling of awakening in the Japanese landscape—the fulfillment of Rexroth's agonizing quest of half a century.

Two short poems follow the long one as a kind of coda linking Christian and Buddhist terminology in renditions of the same basic realization. In "A Song At the Winepresses" for Gary Snyder, Rexroth senses the same love in Mt. Calvary Monastery in Santa Barbara as in Japan (*CLP*, 305). And in "the Spark in the Tinder of Knowing" for James Laughlin, at the Cowley Fathers Monastery in Cambridge, he reaffirms the "Holy Wedding" of existence (*CLP*, 307).

The Collected Longer Poems ends with the aging poet's attainment of spiritual realization in Japan, having begun with the Damascan brothers' youthful quest in upstate New York. As civilization deteriorated after World War I, the wry narrator and speculative brothers of *Homestead* explore through symbols and dialectic the dilemmas of contemplation and action, attaining a kind of Christian-Buddhist resignation. Rexroth does not appear directly in that poem, but in *Prolegomenon* he struggles prophetically through hellish dissociation, both verbal and psychological, into a Beatific Vision that seems more literary than fully realized.

In the "natural numbers" of the remaining three poems he perfected a conversational style for communing with nature and those he loved, and for denouncing the injustices of the "social lie." The theological lover of *The Phoenix and the Tortoise* during World War II, reflecting on the collapse of ancient and modern civilizations, affirms the Integral Person in Community in Buddhist terms of universal interactivity and Christian terms of responsibility through sacramental marriage. The eco-anarcho-Christian-Buddhist philosopher of *The Dragon and the Unicorn*, finding solace in the processes of nature, love, and friendship as he travels through America and Europe, threatened by atomic extinction, expands and concretizes the philosophy of universal love. The Buddhist sage of *The Heart's Garden, The Garden's Heart*, moving beyond dialectical polemics, sinks into the Tao in Japan, compassionately realizing the harmonious interaction of all beings.

Throughout the collection mythic and actual women inspire the poet, often uniting with him in love that spreads through the universe: the elegant Leslie and black stripper Maxine; his wives Marie and Marthe; Lao-tzu's "dark woman of the valley," symbolizing the Tao; the Biblical Lilith and Marichiben, Indian goddess of orgasm and the dawn, appearing in the first and last poems of this volume, and later in the Marichiko sequence. The organic philosophy emerges from erotic mysteries as well as from reverence for landscapes on the west coast, Europe and Japan, under the progressions of planets and constellations, in multiple Buddha-worlds.

New Poems (1974) and *The Morning Star* (1979)

After the major collections of Rexroth's shorter and longer poems came out in the late 1960s, short poems and sequences flowed from his Japanese sojourns into *The Morning Star* (1979), the last book of his original poems issued in his lifetime, consisting of three previously published volumes: *The Silver Swan, On Flower Wreath Hill*, and *The Love Poems of Marichiko*. *New Poems* (1974) is a transition between these books and the previous *The Heart's Garden, The Garden's Heart*, Rexroth's longest poem initiating the predominantly Buddhist outlook that characterizes the final phase of his work.

New Poems (1974)

"Love Is an Art of Time," the opening section of *New Poems* containing the previously published *Sky Sea Birds Trees Earth House Beasts Flowers* and other lyrics, is a reminder that time is organic rather than serial, a major theme in *The Dragon and the Unicorn*; but oriental equanimity has replaced the dialectical polemics of the earlier poem.

Near the end of a sequence of tanka-like lyrics called "The City of the Moon," the Buddha says that out of innumerable truths he has offered only a few, like a handful of autumn leaves (*NP*, 36). In "Void Only," terse allusions yoke two major schools of Mahayana philosophy, the Madyamika of Nagarjuna in which All is Void, and the Yogacara school of Asanga and Vasubandu in which All is Mind (*NP*, 22). In "Suchness," the English equivalent of the Sanskrit Tathata, the soul, like camphor, burns without residue (*NP*, 23). In "Late half moon," Shakyamuni unites with his consort Tara in Tantric union of wisdom and love (*NP*, 24). And in "The Flower Sutra" (*NP*, 26), a Japanese mountain cuckoo cries, "Kegonkyo," the title of the sutra featuring the Net of Indra, foreshadowing *On Flower Wreath Hill*.

The Japanese style is sustained in the selection from the "Marichiko" sequence (published as a whole separately), and in imitations and translations from the Chinese, making *New Poems* more of a sampling of work-in-progress than a unified work.

The Morning Star (1979)

Facing death from a failing heart, Rexroth named *The Morning Star* after the planet that shines forth just before sunrise, a symbol of enlightenment ever since Shakyamuni observed it under the Bo tree about twenty-five centuries ago. The book is the culmination of the poet's lifework and his absorption of Buddha Dharma ever since he had begun translating oriental poetry as a youth.

The Silver Swan (1976)

The first section of *The Morning Star* includes all sixteen of the previously published poems from *The Silver Swan* in 1976, along with twelve new poems and a note. Some of these twenty-eight poems are translations from Günnar Ekelof, the Swedish poet, but all feel Japanese, some are translations from Fujiwara no Taiwa and Japan's greatest woman poet of the twentieth century, Yosano Akiko, and most suggest non-dualities of life and death, mind and nature, past and present, darkness and light, and the one and the many. In the title poem, the complex image of the sleeping swan singing as the moon rises suggests that we may be enlightened when we do not know that we are; and in fact, if we think that we are enlightened, then we have falsely objectified the experience (*MS*, 4).

The moon of enlightenment appears also, in various cycles and seasons, in IV, V, IX, XII, XIII, XVI, XVIII, XIX, XXIII, and climactically in XVII, certainly one of Rexroth's most remarkable poems of ecstatic vision. In it, the poet, like Shakyamuni in nirvana, observes before dawn, near a crescent moon, the Morning Star, which he notes is Marishiten, named after Marishiben, the ancient Indian love-goddess of the dawn who became a bodhisattva for lovers, women in childbirth, prostitutes, geisha, and samurai (*MS*, 85–86). Having inspired him in *The Homestead Called Damascus* and in *The Heart's Garden, The Garden's Heart*, she becomes reincarnated as Marichiko in his final sequence of poems. In XVII, as he walks nude in his Kyoto garden, a ray of the Morning Star becomes the goddess, "Her body made of infinite / Whirling points of light, each one / A galaxy, like clouds of / Fireflies beyond numbering" (*MS*, 19–20). In this complex image, reminiscent of the multiple radiances of Indra's Net, infinite universes are incarnated in her body of light, which flows into the poet's, dissolving illusions of world and self. Awareness ceases in the void of ecstatic love. Then the poet returns to the ordinary world, bathed in the sun of enlightenment, in which star and moon have disappeared.

On Flower Wreath Hill (1976)

The title of the second part of *The Morning Star*, a sequence published as *On Flower Wreath Hill* in 1976, refers both to the *Kegon* sutra, long familiar as the source of Indra's Net, and a Kyoto cemetery near Rexroth's temporary home in Japan, where he prepares for death (*MS*, 83).

This poet-pilgrim on the Middle Way walks through autumn leaves near the grave of an ancient princess who seems to float near him with the ghosts of heroes. As the moon and his guardian constellation Orion rise over the mountain named after the sutra, the reverberations of a temple bell seem never to die, like echoing memories, an aural equivalent of the visual reflections of Indra's Net (*MS*, 39). Because the world is unstable, as the Buddha said on his deathbed, there is only nirvana—nothing to cling to or seek (*MS*, 41). As the poet floats in the living universe like the moon in mist or a child in the womb, his body glows with energy free of the illusions of form (*MS*, 42); or as he explained to me, "Shakti, the Hindu *syzygy* 'power,' in Buddhism is *prajna* 'wisdom,' which obliterates power." As he grows aware that the ephemeral world of change, suffering, and death, of the ephemera of samsara, is also the world of illumination, of nirvana, he envisions a wet "spider's net of jewels" (*MS*, 44–45) as

> the Net of Indra,
> The compound infinities of infinities,
> The Flower Wreath,
> Each universe reflecting
> Every other, reflecting
> Itself from every other,
> And the moon the single thought
> That populates the Void.

As usual, spiritual realization has been brought about erotically, in this sequence through allusions to the Japanese legend of the Weaving Girl who unites for one night only each year with her cowboy lover (symbolized by the stars Vega and Altair in the Tanabata Festival), and to the ancient princess with moon-like eyebrows, who sang for the emperor as she served him wine, one of Rexroth's many muses who keep him on the sacred path (*MS*, 43). Finally, a soundless flute, playing for Krishna's dancing milkmaids, intimates the Tantric Absolute, nirvana in samsara.

The Love Poems of Marichiko (1978)

The Love Poems of Marichiko resemble, in tone and style if not exactly in form, the poems of Yosano Akiko (1878–1942), whose poetry Rexroth translated in several collections and who seems to be a model for Rexroth's invention, Marichiko. He idolized Akiko as the greatest woman poet and love poet of modern Japan. She had revitalized the tanka, inspired feminists and antiwar activists, and edited (with her husband "Tekkan") *Myōjo*, the influential poetry journal of the new romanticism. Translating this title as *The Morning Star*, Rexroth borrowed it for his final book of poems. Like Akiko's famous sequence *Midaregami* (Tangled Hair), the Marichiko poems reveal a tale of the desire of a Japanese woman poet of Buddhist consciousness, blissful union with her lover (III–XXXV), and her desperate longing in separation. Here is Akiko, translated by Rexroth:

> Hair unbound, in this
> Hothouse of lovemaking,
> Perfumed with lilies,
> I dread the oncoming of
> The pale rose of the end of night.[18]

And here is Rexroth's Marichiko in *The Morning Star* (*MS*, 68):

> I cannot forget
> The perfumed dusk inside the
> Tent of my black hair
> As we awoke to make love
> After a long night of love

These poems tell more than a story of a woman's love, for Marichiko seems at times to reincarnate the goddess Marishiben and the Bodhisattva Kannon, as she yearns to embrace her love with a thousand arms; and her indistinct lover seems to be Dainichi Nyorai, the universal Buddha symbolized by the sun. So the story may be read as a kind of Tantric parable of contemplative ecstacy, traditionally symbolized by the sexual union of lovers.[19]

From the first poem on, Marichiko's desire and longing exemplify the Buddha's First Noble Truth, that suffering results from attachments. She is so disoriented by passion that space is distorted (II) and she babbles nonsense to her lover, whom we never clearly see (III). Sometimes, united, they are peaceful (XI), but often desire seems unquenchable (VII); then, when the Morning Star shines, all things light up with love (VIII). In erotic enlightenment she exclaims that he awakens her (IX). Watching fires in the shape of the Japanese character for "big" burn on Daimonji Mountain near Kyoto on August 16, she echoes the Buddha's Fire Sermon, but seems to forget that even their great love will be eventuallly consumed (XIV: see also the heart-fires in XVIII). XX is like a Zen koan, in which she is lost to her lover, just as Rexroth and the reader have lost themselves in her. In XXI the stars reflect Indra's Net; in XXII the Morning Star (Marishiten) glows over the ocean of the universe (and in XXX it illuminates the world); in XXIII Marichiko wants to be Kannon Bodhisattva of eleven heads and a thousand arms to embrace him; and in XXVI the sun and moon of enlightenment (from *The Flower Wreath Sutra*) appear. Holding her lover's head between her thighs, she floats on the River of Heaven (the Milky Way, XXXII). After flooding light implies the union of the pre-Buddhist goddess Marishiben with the universal Buddha Dainichi Nyorai (Mahavairocana, symbolized by the sun), suddenly in XXXVI Marichiko's lover departs as shadowy as when he came (III)—as if enlightenment were as temporary as all other phenomena.

Alone, she is perishing (LIV). In union, she was Dainichi's wisdom; but apart, the lover changes like the universe itself. She faces death, hating daylight, a reminder of ecstatic enlightenment which passes like everything else. In XLII she is fated to love without attaining final enlightenment. In XLV she had innocently presumed that her own love would continue forever, when she had watched with her lover a No play about the dancer Shizuka Gozen, fated lover of the great warrior Yoshitsune.

Who is Marishiko's mysterious lover? As if he might be pure spirit there is doubt that she actually sees him or even his shadow; and yet he has flesh enough to hold her breasts, kiss her thighs, tongue her, and bite her nipples. He also writes poems in love letters. In XLVI (and the note on p. 88) she thinks that he is Dainichi Nyorai, the universal Buddha of Shingon (Tantric) Buddhism, identified with the sun; but since Buddha-nature is in all of us, he may be any man, enlightened when united with her, when she was his wisdom, like Prajnaparamita (the female incarnation of Perfect Wisdom) sexually united with the Buddha in Tantric *yabyum*. Lost from her, her lover is shadowy and ghostly (LIX). Her love turns to hate as she remembers how his gaze froze her like the moon at dawn (LX). She has returned from nirvana to samsara instead of realizing that nirvana and samsara are inseparable.

Rexroth's extensive notes, like Eliot's for *The Waste Land*, are as puzzling as they are useful. In his last letter to me, on March 15, 1979, he wrote that

The poem "breaks" at the moments of hubris, watching the fiery 大 from the Kamogawa Bridge and at the Shizoka Gozen poem, where she realizes that illumination has been corrupted by *hubris*. It is the same plot as my plays—except *Iphigenia*.

As usual, Rexroth's cross-cultural insights are ingenious. Hubris in the Greek sense of overweening pride does not enter Buddhism, in which self-conscious attachments are manifestations of ignorance of nirvana. By bringing a Japanese woman to hubris, Rexroth develops her character towards the tragic intensity of *Beyond the Mountains*, well beyond the conventions of tanka and No, in which a heroine would be resigned, no matter how miserable. It is as if a Japanese woman agonizes with desire and despair in a play by Euripides.

Marichiko is Rexroth's most enigmatic work. Was he using Buddhist traditions primarily to write love poems, or does he join the ranks of great contemplative poets, symbolizing the experience of nirvana in sexual union? Or both? Does Marichiko reflect Rexroth's failure to attain permanent enlightenment, his confusion of it with eros, the recognition of his own hubris, his failure to practice strict Tantric disciplines in which sexual meditation is a highly controlled "skillful means," not to be confused with Marichiko's abandon? And who, finally, is Marichiko?

She is, I think, the distillation of all of Rexroth's lovers as well as his anima, the feminine, yin aspect of his personality, a personification of his creative imagination, in which the lone self is lost in the poetic process of uniting beings who appear to be separate. Akiko-Marichiko enters Rexroth's pantheon of muse-saviors, joining his wives, lovers, women of Artemis in the plays, ancient poets, heroines, and his mother. All of them, rising from nature and embodying wisdom, inspired his poetry of spiritual realization. Through contemplative union with them, realizing the interdependency of all beings, he passed into the great nirvana of death but continues to live and speak in his poetry, which remains for us a way of waking up.

The Morning Star is Rexroth's "death and transfiguration." In it, *The Silver Swan* commemorates the death of others and his absorption into the spirit of the Morning Star; approaching death on Flower Wreath Hill, among ghosts of heroes and princesses, he envisions the

Net of Indra as a spider-web; and in the finale, he is transformed into Marichiko. Having found himself, he loses himself in her.

Whether we read Rexroth's poems sequentially from book to book, attending to his artistic and philosophical development, or randomly as we are drawn to favorite poems, let us not forget that studying them is but preparation for reading aloud in direct communication to others. As he never tired of reminding us, poems are music to be performed: the text is a score for speaking them and hearing them, person to person, in the re-creation of community. Public performances of poetry thus become commemorations of the poet, friendships, affections, heroic acts. Communing with him in the poems as he loves and protests, thinks and acts in the world, and perhaps leaves it in transcendent ecstacies, we become more fully human; our feelings are enriched and our minds expanded, perhaps into countless Buddha-worlds.

The Plays: *Beyond the Mountains* (1951)

Rexroth's poetic, philosophical, and visionary powers are epitomized in the dramatic tetralogy *Beyond the Mountains* in which he communicates more profoundly than in any other work love as universal responsibility and the integral person as the center of community. Here, tragic conflicts among Greek heroes and heroines openly work out the abstract dialectical personalism of *The Dragon and the Unicorn*. Thanks to the passionate and precise direct address, in lines usually varying from seven to nine syllables, the characters, much more substantially developed than the Damascan brothers in *Homestead*, speak heroically without being bombastic. Iphigenia, Hippolytus, Phaedra, and others achieve transcendence through mysteries of erotic union and sacrificial death, which had enticed but eluded the Damascan youths and which Rexroth had talked about at length in the other long poems.

Rexroth acknowledged the influence of No drama, ritual verse-plays in which masked actors chant their lines, subtly gesture, and dance, but his plays resemble Euripidean tragedy much more closely than the highly elusive and less logically structured Japanese plays or than Yeats's *Plays for Dancers*, which had given Rexroth an early impression of No in Chicago.[1] Rexroth's characters argue much more persistently and intellectually than do the more shadowy Japanese and Irish characters. As in both Greek and Japanese theater, dances evoke the sexual ecstacy of Phaedra and Hippolytus and, at the end of the tetralogy, the collapse of classical civilization. In the plays are two choruses, the first consisting of a young prostitute and beggar whose curious resemblances to various heroines and heroes is a reminder that tragic figures emerge from, and return to, the common people. At the conclusion of the tetralogy, the beggar changes roles with Menander, and the prostitute with Berenike. The second chorus, throughout, consists of four musicians who act also as populace, commentators, and stage hands (*BM*, 14).

If Rexroth's plays seem more Greek than Japanese in form and ideas, they nevertheless reflect the Buddhism of No explicitly and implicitly. The choruses, including bald beggars holding bowls like monks, repeat some of Shakyamuni's last words concerning the ephemerality of the world (*BM*, 67). The Buddha's Fire Sermon is transformed into Hippolytus's erotic speech to Phaedra about their union spraying fire that burns down the world (*BM*, 47). In fact, Hippolytus's intention before being seduced by Phaedra is to retire like a monk from the world that his father has corrupted. Vowing to take no life, he worships the goddess Artemis, who seems to be identified as Avalokiteshvara (Kannon), the Bodhisattva of Compassion who traditionally hears "the world's cry," a phrase Rexroth applies to Artemis (*BM*, 21). Menander, who in the tetralogy is the last Greek king eventually destroyed by the Huns, is modeled on a Bactrian philosopher-king who was converted to Buddhism by the sage Nagasena.[2] In *Berenike* Menander echoes *The Flower Wreath Sutra* in lines that suggest the Net of Indra, which Rexroth creatively transforms into a "cobweb" of infinite lines imagined between stars; and the mutually reflecting mirrors of the sutra become infinite pairs of lovers whose eyes reflect each other (*BM*, 158–59):

> I have no real being.
> I am like an astronomer's
> Imaginary line, just one
> Probable strand in your cobweb
> Of the infinite possible,
> And so you are to me. Millions
> Times millions Menanders
> Face the unending mirrors of
> Berenikes at this instant,
> And a million times a million
> Berenikes see themselves in
> The firelit pupils of their brothers,
> As I see myself in your eyes.

Finally, enlightenment is imaged in the climactic dance of light.

Another important quality of Buddhism and No found in

Beyond the Mountains is *yūgen*, a term derived from Zen that means subtlety, often symbolized by a white bird carrying a flower.[3] Although the tetrology is full of *yūgen*, perhaps it is most apparent in the epigram spoken by the First Chorus in *Berenike*: "We meet and touch and pass on/As log meets log in mid-ocean" (*BM*, 189).

Some of Rexroth's characters are derived from Euripides, but they are transformed with the kind of moral clarity that we associate more with Sophocles's heroes. In *Classics Revisited*, Rexroth distinguishes between Sophocles's tragedies of will and fate and Euripides' tragi-comedies in which egoists are trapped in confusion.[4] In Rexroth's plays, cynical men of the world such as Demetrios, Theseus, and Agamemnon are treated as Euripides would have presented them, as mock-heroic parodies. Their motives are debased by their vulgarity, sentimentality, and callousness. On the other hand, Rexroth treats women of Artemis such as Iphigenia and Phaedra, and their lovers Achilles and Hippolytus, as Sophocles would have conceived them, ennobled by their suffering. Their fate is their responsibility, not the result of an external cause of catastrophe. In moral triumph and physical defeat they struggle with universalizing love, and their sacrifice renews community.

Phaedra

Phaedra, the first play, depends upon Euripides' *Hippolytus*, but Rexroth radically transformed the main characters and made explicit the fertility ritual from which Greek tragedy emerged (*BM*, 16). As King Theseus commits adultery with Persephone in Hades, Phaedra rages against the Greeks who had savagely killed her father, King Minos, smashed Crete, kidnapped her, and made her a princess to reproduce her flesh. In fury she performs the Minotaur dance, the fertility rite on which Cretan civilization depends; but alone, she is powerless, mad, sterile. Meanwhile, her stepson Hippolytus, abandoning his princely duty to father new armies, has become an ascetic seeking visions of Artemis (*BM*, 18).

In Euripides' play, a Nurse-confidante, to whom Phaedra admits her love for Hippolytus, betrays the secret to him; and self-righteously rejecting her, he is falsely condemned by his father. But Rexroth drops the Nurse; and perhaps influenced by the possibility of a lost earlier version by Euripides in which Phaedra directly proposes to Hippolytus,[5] he has Hippolytus falling into her arms as if she is Artemis. When they part, she predicts that they will pay for this crime, alluding to Proudhon's "property is theft" (*BM*, 39). Hippolytus is naively optimistic, but she knows that Theseus will find them out. They are not simply victims of vengeful Aphrodite, as in Euripides' version, but are doomed by their sense of responsibility.

Hippolytus momentarily regrets their mortal love which has prevented him from attaining immortal union with Artemis, but Phaedra persuades him that he had attained salvation in her arms, and there is more than a suggestion that she is the goddess incarnate, for she weeps for the world, and when she asks him if he would recognize Artemis, he turns dead white (*BM*, 34–35). Even after accepting her love, he has difficulty accepting the consequences. He does not understand her insistence that vision is "evisceration" (*BM*, 42); and as her speech becomes more paradoxical, he wants to unite with just a woman, not with nothingness (*BM*, 44). Suddenly abandoning responsibility, she invites him to escape to a utopian colony in Italy; but renouncing political leadership he accepts their love, regardless of the consequences. She agrees, uttering the cruel paradox that now is never (*BM*, 47). They drink sacramental wine, dance again, and the Chorus hymns their love. Nevertheless, impure intentions destroy them (*BM*, 9); or as the Chorus concludes the play, "Each sinned with each other's virtue" (*BM*, 55).

When Theseus returns from Hades, Phaedra commits suicide, and the matured Hippolytus courageously confronts him, expecting horror and wrath. But unlike the suspicious, grief-struck, vengeful Theseus of Euripides' play, Rexroth's Theseus cynically tells his son that he planned even their incest and adultery to satisfy them during his absence. Euripides has Hippolytus, a self-righteous virgin, condemned to unjust banishment, smashed in his chariot, chased by a bull; whereas Rexroth's hero is trampled to death by the bull on which his father has ridden from Hades. Despite impurity of intention, Rexroth's couple achieves transcendence through perfect erotic union and sacrifical death, the fulfillment of the dreams of *Homestead*. At the end, instead of Artemis's bringing Theseus to enlightenment, remorse, and final reconciliation with his dying son, as in the original play, Rexroth's Theseus, incapable of moral responsibility, banally wonders why trouble comes his way.

Iphigenia at Aulis

In Euripides' *Iphigenia at Aulis*, the heroine's father Agamemnon invites her and her mother Clytemnestra to come from Argos to

Aulis, where the Greek ships are becalmed, for the ostensible purpose of marrying her to Achilles; but actually she is to be sacrificed to Artemis, who will blow the ships to Troy. When Iphigenia discovers his real purpose, she at first pleads with him, but later resolves to die for glory for saving Greece.[6] In Rexroth's version, however, she has initiated the idea of her sacrifice, but for three months her father has resisted her offer. Loving her more than his Euripidean counterpart loved her counterpart, he is, in fact, her lover, and he tells her that she is worth more than any victory. Nevertheless, as a man of the world who believes that they are fated (or karmically determined), he allows her to persuade him (*BM*, 67). Ironically, she uses arguments that he had used in Euripides' play. Ironically also, he is more concerned about his own guilt than about her death. Meanwhile, celebrating a perfect union with her true love, Achilles, she tells him that she has no being but him; but their love cannot prevent her from sacrificing herself for the pure act (*BM*, 70–73). In her acts of love and sacrifice, she becomes Artemis herself (*BM*, 80). She dances ecstatically with Agamemnon, who knows that she will die, and with Achilles, who despite his wisdom believes that they can be reunited after the war. As Agamemnon kills Iphigenia offstage, the Chorus concludes the play with prophetic lines that are reminiscent of Yeats's prophecy of another Troy rising and setting, at the finale of *The Resurrection*.[7] Rexroth's lines are (*BM*, 91):

> The flames crawl over Troy's walls.
> Asia falls into ruins.
> Aeneas and Odysseus
> Wander, lost in a new world.
> Helen dies in a brothel.

The characters of *Iphigenia at Aulis* are wiser than those of the first play. Agamemnon is a more sensitive man than Theseus; Achilles, more aware of the consequences of love than Hippolytus, escapes his tragic death; and Iphigenia's motives are the purest of any in the tetralogy.

Hermaios

Like Yeats's *Resurrection*, Rexroth's last two plays ritualize the transition from pagan to Christian culture. Yeats saw a virgin replace Dionysus[8]; and Rexroth's Chorus at the beginning of *Hermaios*, which takes place in the last Greek stronghold on the night before Christ's birth, prophesies that a bloody baby will replace the erotic Greek deities (*BM*, 95, 101).

Hermaios Soter, utopian ruler of the last independent Greek city state (in Bactria, Afghanistan), agrees with the Magi that a new god is being born; but instead of accompanying them to Bethlehem, he has been trying to appease a gang of Huns in order to preserve his bastion of classical culture. Betrayed by them, he has temporarily fought them off with the help of his heroic mistress, an Indian named Tarakaia who worships Artemis in trances. Kalliope, who is both his wife and sister, urges him to escape to Rome, but he proudly lashes imperial decadence and instead proposes to realize a Platonic utopia (*BM*, 125–26). Demetrios, who is at once Kalliope's brother and lover, seems to agree with him, but they betray both Hermaios and Tarakaia, who die with dignified foreknowledge as smooth-talking Demetrius takes over.

Hermaios achieves transcendence by virtue of his utopian commitment, but it is limited by ego and will, as was classical culture generally: so this last Greek humanist dies for nothing new. Certain that he has made the wisest possible decision, he lacks the universal compassion of Tarakaia, who might have responded to Christianity despite the ferocity of her fighting the Huns.

Berenike

The Chorus in the final play, *Berenike*, watching over the bodies of Hermaios and Tarakaia, expresses the doctrine of total responsibility that Rexroth develops more expansively in *The Phoenix and the Tortoise* and *The Dragon and the Unicorn* (*BM*, 150). Hermaios's daughter Berenike vows vengeance against the usurpers Demetrios and Kalliope; but her brother Menander, who is even more passive and withdrawn than Hippolytus, tells her that she is caught in the web of karma, from which he wants only to escape (*BM*, 152), a Buddhist wish to escape samsara for nirvana. Berenike, who is even more willful than Phaedra, replies (*BM*, 154):

> You are blind.
> The door to inaction is called
> Action, and the gate of action
> Is called inaction. You cannot
> Find bliss by dropping your eyelids.

She begs Menander to use her to avenge their father's death, but he denies that he has will, judgment, fire, being. She persists, sword-dancing, joining with him ecstatically as Phaedra and Hippolytus danced, but he continues to be passive. So she turns to Demetrios and, seducing him, stabs him as they dance. He dies cynically, and she foresees the inevitable end of herself and the classical world. Menander nevertheless still refuses to act, and the Chorus agrees that in the illusory world means are distinct from ends, but in reality an act is its own end (*BM*, 181).

As Berenike dances, the Chorus announces the end of the Greek era and sings the first Delphic hymn. Sword in hand, Menander confronts Kalliope but dares not take vengeance. Accepting full responsibility for her crimes, she knows that history, or fate, will move the sword from his hand to her heart; and it does just that as the Chorus announces the birth of Christ. Acting in spite of himself, Menander loses the moral purity he had tried so carefully to preserve. Kalliope achieves transcendence by taking responsibility for her acts, whereas he does not even die. Instead, through complicated dance movements at the finale of the tetralogy, they take the places of beggar and prostitute in the First Chorus as the Huns rush in for the massacre.

In Rexroth's plays one human type is the destructive man of the world, such as Theseus (who cynically lets Athens sicken while he visits Persephone in Hades), the usurper Demetrios, and Agamemnon (who sacrifices his daughter Iphigenia despite his knowledge that victory over Troy will not be worth the price).

Transcending the unjust world, on the other hand, are certain women who worship Artemis (*BM*, 32). Iphigenia, the most saintly of all Rexroth's characters, beyond dualities of cause and effect, will and purpose, persuades Agamemnon to sacrifice her to Artemis (*BM*, 74). Phaedra gives herself completely to the fires of creative process, but kills herself out of fear as well as responsibility. Tarakaia, whose compassion extends to mankind despite her violence, ranks higher on a scale of transcendence than Kalliope, who merely accepts guilt, or Berenike, who seduces Demetrios in order to kill him in vengeance.

Male counterparts of the women of Artemis, inspired by them but less charismatic, try to detach themselves from the world like the

Damascan brothers, but with varying degrees of certainty. Torn between the human love of Phaedra and the divine love of the goddess, Hippolytus burns more brightly than Hermaios, whose good intentions are to make a good society rather than to transcend it; so he remains in the world of purpose. Achilles is guilt-ridden because of his consuming love for Iphigenia, and Menander tries to escape responsibility for the death of his mother.

Though motives are humanly impure, these men and women achieve various degrees of transcendence, some helping to create community in the face of depersonalizing forces, not only from Huns but from cynical Greek rulers as well. Depending on the purity of action, the integral person accepts responsibility. No act in the plays is explicitly Christian or Buddhist, but universal compassion, love, responsible sacrifice, and utopianism are essential ingredients of both religions. Demetrios, Theseus, and Agamemnon still rule the world, and acts of sacrificial love in our warlike world still reflect the values of these plays and the spiritual traditions embodied in them.

Beyond the Mountains is Rexroth's most fully realized literary work. It must be understood and performed not only as drama and poetry but fundamentally as sacrament that renews our sense of integral persons as the source of true community, arising from mysterious processes of creation and destruction but ultimately transcending them. The flexibility of Rexroth's style perfectly generates a range of characters as psychologically and as morally complex as their classical counterparts. Shall we strive for power or withdraw into the contemplative life? Is love salvation or deception? How can we be one with another, with humankind, with the universe? The answers come, if at all, not through reason, but through the poetry of these plays.

5

Translation as an "Act of Sympathy"

Rexroth objected to distinguishing "original" poems from translations, for they both sprang from the same imaginative interaction with poets, ancient and modern, from around the world. Allusions, imitations, and other adaptations of their work echo throughout poems and plays that are very much his own, shaping style, technique, and themes, and contributing to his complex worldview in which the vast influence of religious and philosophical literature is originally synthesized. His cubism is indebted to Reverdy and other French poets, for example, and his characteristic technique of direct address is shaped, in part, by western classical poetry as well as by such oriental forms as tanka, haiku, No, koan, gatha, and the sutras.

Nevertheless, he did separate out translations in thirteen collections as well as in sections in volumes of shorter poems. Only an expert in Latin, Greek, Chinese, Japanese, French, and Spanish can properly evaluate his translations as a whole. How accurately do they reflect the meaning, tone, sound, and implications of the originals? How did various languages affect his feelings and attitudes about places, people, and ideas? How reliably do his translations introduce us to the nuances of unfamiliar literatures and civilizations? Those important questions cannot be answered here, but a general approach to Rexroth's translations in terms of his literary philosophy may help multilingual critics as well as general readers.

Though accuracy is one function of translation, it is not the most important. Rexroth called translation "an act of sympathy" in which one poet identifies with another, transferring the other's speech to his own.[1] Ever since he was fifteen, imaginary conversations with Sappho, Tu Fu, Martial, and other poets brought him into their worlds as he comprehended their inner lives as well as their artistry. Translation for him was, then, like the creation of all art, an act of sacred contemplation, a compassionate ritual of incarnation, a reminder that the universe itself is the perpetual translation of forms of energy. Such universal transformation is symbolized most eloquently in *The Lotus Sutra*, the Chinese classic in which the great Bodhisattva of Compassion, Avalokiteshvara of many faces and arms, changes into infinitely various forms that express no-form, the formless form of Buddha-nature. Like a Bodhisattva, Rexroth became oriental as well as European, and feminine in his versions of Yosano Akiko, Ono no Komachi, and Li Ch'ing Chao, changing into countless persons, styles, and forms as "skillful means" of transmitting wisdom.

How faithfully Rexroth renders the character of a poet in a particular translation can be judged reliably only by a critic as sympathetically insightful as himself. Literalists who tolerate only pedantic equivalence cannot appreciate Rexroth's versions, or Pound's, or any truly creative translation. Of course there are bound to be inaccuracies; of course there is always Rexroth's voice, just as the voice of a versatile actor "becomes" Hamlet's voice, so we imagine Hamlet while appreciating the actor. Some readers object to Rexroth's idiosyncrasies, and sometimes these do get in the way; but more often they help project the unique tone and outlook of poets as diverse as Meleager and Hitomaro against the figured bass of the translator's voice; so readers generally seem to share the excitement of his discovery of many great poets and their work that is conveyed through his own.

Most importantly, his translations are exemplary works of art in their own right, English poems that can be thoroughly appreciated without concern for accuracy, just as Pound's "River Merchant's Wife" and Fitzgerald's "Rubaiyat" are part of our own literature, cherished by those who have no knowledge of Chinese or Persian. Even as the Marichiko hoax proves that "her" poems require no knowledge of Japanese "originals," so translations must be judged as autonomous works of art, regardless of their relationship to work in other languages.

Rexroth's sensitivity and erudition as a translator were widely appreciated from the mid-1950s on after the ever-popular *One Hundred Poems from the Japanese (PJ)* came out. His introduction states that Japanese poetry depends primarily on sensibility rather than on the rhetoric and decoration so familiar in western poetry (*PJ*, ix). So there are incredibly intense insights in short poems such as "A strange old man / Stops me / Looking out of my deep mirror" (Hitomaro, *PJ*, 24). This volume and *One Hundred More Poems from the Japanese (More PJ)*, cover the whole tradition from the Eighth Century *Manyoshu* into our own century, with copious notes and bibliographies. The compassionate sadness of solitude, loss, disillusionment, and dreamy yearning known as *mono-no-aware*, the prevailing tone of Japanese Buddhism, is conveyed in perfectly natural English in poem after poem. The dark path in a poem by Izamu Shikibu suggests the obscurities of the Buddha's Way (*More PJ*, 27). Comparing the world to the white wake of a boat at dawn, the monk Shami Manei suggests insubstantiality, nothingness, void (*More PJ*, 36). And though Rexroth disliked the sentimentality of most haiku, he cherished Bashō's, which he saw no need to render in the 5-7-5 syllables that are perfectly natural in Japanese but constricting in English. There is also Shiki's "Fresh from the Void," in which the moon rises from the sea (*More PJ*, 109)—a favorite image that also enters *The Phoenix and the Tortoise*, *The Silver Swan*, and other original works by Rexroth as well.

Feeling that the poetry of Japanese women was not sufficiently known, he collaborated with a leading Tokyo feminist, Ikuko Atsumi, in translations collected in *The Burning Heart: Women Poets of Japan*, and with her and others in *Seasons of Sacred Lust: Selected Poems of Kazuko Shiraishi*, Japan's most famous living woman poet whose rebel-ways, atypical of Japanese women, are suggested by the beginning of a poem about her Canadian origins, in which she shoots at the face of her country because she loves it (p. 11).

Similarly, Rexroth promoted the work of Chinese women in *The Orchid Boat: Women Poets of China* and *Li Ch'ing Chao Complete Poems*, both books done in collaboration with the Chinese poet Ling Chung. But first he had issued *One Hundred Poems from the Chinese (PC)* three decades after he had begun translating Tu Fu, his favorite nondramatic, nonepic poet from all literatures. Coming through more vividly as a whole person than any other poet in the translations, Tu Fu most resembles Rexroth in cherishing friendships, loving

nature, speaking out against injustice, and suffering with all humanity, especially in wartime. These qualities are embodied in the conclusion of "Night in the House by the River" (*PC*, 33):

> Over the Triple Gorge the Milky Way
> Pulsates between the stars.
> The bitter cries of thousands of households
> Can be heard above the noise of battle.
> Everywhere the workers sing wild songs.
> The great heroes and generals of old time
> Are yellow dust forever now.
> Such are the affairs of men.
> Poetry and letters
> Persist in silence and solitude.

The epigrammatic, sometimes tendentious conclusion of many
poems is one of several common characteristics of both poets, as in
Tu Fu's "Away, I become like you, / An empty boat, floating, adrift"
or "Life whirls past like drunken wildfire" (*PC*, 4–5). And a long,
eloquent note explains how Tu Fu's poetry improved Rexroth morally and psychologically (*PC*, 149). Also in this volume are poems of
the Sung Dynasty, randomly selected as they pleased him, and
generally sweeter, more romantic, less engaged in humanity's suffering than Tu Fu's.

In *Love and the Turning Year: One Hundred More Poems from the
Chinese*, Rexroth goes back to some of the earliest folk songs from
The Book of Odes, then includes samples from various centuries. A
notable omission is Li Po, perhaps because of the preeminence of
Pound's versions.

Turning to Western classics, we find in *Poems from the Greek
Anthology* a few from Latin, such as the excerpt from the "Carmina
Burana," possibly by Abelard, and terse, tough satires of Martial and
Petronius, as well as the majority from Greek. All are in natural
speech that brings these poets back to life. *Thirty Spanish Poems of
Love and Exile* is an anarchist's choice of modern lyrics by Alberti,
Guillen, Lorca, Machado, and climactically, Neruda.

There are three collections from French. *Fourteen Poems by O. V.
de L. Milosz*, the first book of translations that Rexroth published,
contains poems of daily life in Paris by this poet who had been a
Lithuanian official after World War I. *One Hundred Poems from the*

French is also from the modern period—Artaud, Carco, Char, Cros, Goll, Supervielle, Reverdy, and others who affected the symbolist and cubist modes of Rexroth's poetry before World War II—along with three poems from Medieval Provençal. The cubist Reverdy influenced him more than anyone in England or America, according to his introduction to *Pierre Reverdy Selected Poems*, his most spirited defense of the Revolution of the Word; and "A Ringing Bell" shows that cubism may be tender as well as tough (p. 15).

Besides being delightful as individual poems, Rexroth's translations are moments of interpersonal communion transmitting wisdom across frontiers that normally divide languages, literatures, and civilizations. His translations as a whole, combining vast traditions of East and West, show us the world in an extension of the pioneering work by Pound, Hearn, Waley, and others. They are essential units in Rexroth's worldview, in which each being reflects every other, just as a Japanese teardrop reflects our loneliness.

6

Rexroth As Culture-Critic

Because Rexroth was a philosophical poet, his theory of literature emerged directly from his practice; his essays extend the thinking of his poetry, offering an antidote to the depersonalizing jargon of much current criticism. His own criticism had packed wallop after wallop against the "social lie" and for revolutionary artistic truth since the 1930s, but *Bird in the Bush: Obvious Essays (BB)*, his first collection, did not appear until 1959, the title alluding to the jazz great Charley Parker. Rexroth called his prose intellectual journalism like that of Huneker, Mencken, Wilson, and he might have added Herbert Read and Albert Camus. He blistered Henry James, Kierkegaard, Dostoyevsky, Beat poets, Cold Warriors, and pedants. With off-beat insights and erudite polemics, he celebrated the fiction of ancient China and Japan, Mark Twain and Henry Miller, the plays of Yeats and Beckett, the poetry of Lawrence and Patchen, the paintings of Turner and Morris Graves, jazz and the I-Thou of Martin Buber. In prose as in poetry, a prophetic voice awakens the reader with sarcasm and epigrams:

> The hipster is the furious square. (*BB*, 40)
> Genuine revolt goes with an all-too-definite life aim—
> hardly with the lack of it. (*BB*, 43)
> Heroism is only smouldering and will flame up after all
> these dark ages are over. (*BB*, 84)

Always full of surprises, he slides mind-boggling ideas into subordinate clauses as afterthoughts, or summarizes centuries of Christian, Jewish, or Buddhist thought as if it were as familiar as the story of his own life. Often it *is* the story of his life, for he absorbed and tested whatever he studied, trying it out intellectually, emotionally, and practically, trying to meditate like Lao-tzu or painting like Sesshu, for instance. He wrote from the inside of what he wrote about, inspiring the reader to enter the creative adventure also. His claims are sometimes extravagant and always debatable, but his writing shines through much of the fog that hangs over literature.

In *Assays*, interpretations of Chinese culture, the Kaballah and Gnosticism, American Indian songs, translation, youth revolt, and American poetry expand themes introduced in the first collection, the contemplative, communicative, and communal functions of art. *Classics Revisited* and "More Classics Revisited" in *The Elastic Retort*, essays reprinted from *Saturday Review*, comprise a comprehensive introduction to world literature, going beyond the European limitations of the Hutchins–Adler Great Books. Also in *The Elastic Retort* are sections on Japan, ancient and modern, and Christian theology. *The Alternative Society* focuses on recent American writing in relation to the mentality of permanent war. *With Eye and Ear* covers the Far East, Christianity, world classics, and American writing with versatility, though these essays are not as startling as the earlier ones. *American Poetry in the Twentieth Century* analyzes literary interactions among such communities as the Indian, Spanish, French, German, English, Protestant, Catholic, Jewish, Chinese, Japanese, and Negro, regional groups such as New England transcendentalists and Southern agrarians, the Midwestern and West Coast renaissances, and movements such as imagism, cubism, Marxism, and the Beats, never failing to point up unique achievements of individual poets, though judgments are frequently reductive.

In his longest study, *Communalism: from Its Origins to the Twentieth Century*, Rexroth examines bizarre, chaotic, and sometimes immoral but always idealistic attempts to re-create communities of free-association (p. lx), the "Libertarian Tradition" from the Neolithic Village, through Christian mysticism and some Near Eastern and Russian communities, into more than a century of American utopianism that culminates in the "Post-Apocalyptic Communalism" of the 1960s (p. 229). Those communes have been the most successful, ethically and practically, he claims, that have been held together by powerful religious or ideological commitments, charismatic leaders, well-planned divisions of labor, and ceremonial celebrations of life.

This historical study clarifies many ideas alluded to, sometimes enigmatically, in his poetry, and helps to justify his worldview. However, there is no evidence that he ever lived in a commune after deciding against a religious vocation in his youth. Rather than retreating into a local utopia, he arrived at the mystical insight that people are naturally in a universal community of interdependent beings that is revealed and improved by world-wide networks of artists, thinkers, revolutionaries, saints, and Bodhisattvas. Vision evolves from this preexisting community, creates poems and other forms of communication, and liberates and transforms persons. So vision evolves from community and recreates community. Humanistic revolution is the development of transpersonal values inherent in the universal community of beings, whereas collectivism is coercively depersonalizing, in his view. Communitarian personalism kept him free of the authoritarian Left and Right and of American capitalism disguised as democracy. He held out for liberty, compassionate action, voluntary association, mutual aid, and a community of love arising from I-Thou communion. He prophetically denounced alienation, exploitation, power-madness, violence, war most of all, and refused to compromise his vision.

Out of his family's radical heritage he had, as a child, committed himself to the liberation of humanity, later participating in the Revolution of the Word, and of the Deed. But his optimism was dashed by World War I. Though much serious postwar literature signaled the collapse of the idea of progress, he nevertheless retained some hope for social and cultural revolution. Like Trotsky, he thought that the Russian Revolution had been betrayed; but he believed it had been betrayed by Trotsky as well as by Stalin and Lenin—by bolshevism, which had violently and dictatorially violated the I-Thou of personal trust, love, and responsibility no less than had capitalistic "democracy." Inspired by Bakunin, Kropotkin, Tolstoy, Emma Goldman, and Spanish syndicalists, he swam in the mainstream of anarchism, which was not for him merely activism against state-power, but a mystical movement of interpersonal realization of universal responsibility for all beings, nonhuman and human. So anarchism blended nondualistically with ecology, Christian mysticism, and Buddhism.

Distrusting systems of all kinds, Rexroth did not write a definitive prose work philosophically uniting the major dimensions of his worldview, which are drawn together in his poetry more intricately than in his prose. For a clearer and more detailed sense of his intellectual development, we need a collection of his most important introductions, some to volumes of his own work and some to his editions of the work of others, along with hitherto unpublished prose. His introduction to *The New British Poets* for instance, offers an ever-fresh "neo-romantic" alternative to the impersonality of much modernism. And one of his last essays, the introduction to *The Buddhist Writings of Lafcadio Hearn*, offers a concise exposition of Japanese Buddhism that illuminates his own poetry. Rexroth might well be praised as he praised Hearn, for helping to prepare the West for the Japanese sense of nature and of Dharma (p. 27), so vital in the wisdom of Rexroth's poetry and prose.

And what is wisdom? Since ancient times in Asia and in the West wisdom has meant not mere learning, but profound insight or realization of life and death in the double sense of creating as well as understanding reality and truth. Out of favor in our technocratic age, wisdom has never been needed more than today. More than most modern poets, the work of Kenneth Rexroth transmits wisdom from what the Japanese call *Kokoro*—the one heart-mind that is all and yet nothing.

Now that Rexroth's poetry, translations, essays, autobiography, and ideas can be understood in the context of his lifework and world-vision as a whole, many specialized aspects of Rexroth's art can be explored more satisfactorily than ever before: relations between his painting and poetry, oral and written dimensions of his poetry, artistic and intellectual influences of all kinds, prosody, and his achievement relative to that of other poets, to mention only a few. New editions of his writings being prepared by Bradford Morrow will include hitherto unpublished work from the University of California at Los Angeles and the University of Southern California. The rest of his autobiography is needed as well as a biography that evaluates the accuracy of his self-image in the context of the actual events of his life.

Cultural interpretation and evaluation is endless, for the dogmas, canons, methodologies, and judgments of each age are replaced in the next. If this study does nothing else, may it alert readers to the enduring importance of Rexroth, his writings, and his ideas. I have tried to show how some of his poems are true as well as beautiful, how he thought as well as felt deeply, how his art can change minds as well as hearts, and how it can enrich our sense of the creative process of the universe.

In concluding my first book on Rexroth, I compared his outlook with that of George Santayana, Susanne Langer, Denis Seurat, and others concerned with philosophical poetry by Spenser, Milton, Goethe, Nietzsche, Blake, Whitman, Yeats, and others (*Kenneth Rexroth*, 128–32). Since then it has become apparent that phenomenological and hermeneutical critics are likely to find Rexroth's poetic theory and practice congenial. Rexroth's vision is of "being - in-the-world," to quote Heidegger without implying that Rexroth was influenced by him. Like Schleiermacher, Rexroth assumed that understanding rests upon preunderstanding (in community), rather than upon the objective interpretation of signs. Like Wittgenstein, Rexroth saw through the games of language by focusing on "lifeforms." Like Gadamer, he dialectically questioned poems, letting them speak out of their traditions instead of imposing methodological categories on them. Structuralist, semiotic, deconstructive, and other linguistically oriented critics and "language poets" have much to contribute to an understanding of Rexroth's cubist innovations. For Freudians and Jungians there is his erotic symbolism. And his absorption and interpretations of diverse cultures harmonize with the ethnopoetics of Rothenberg, Tarn, and others.

But among modern philosophical currents in the West, the process philosophy of Alfred North Whitehead, Charles Hartshorne, Nolan Pliny Jacobson, and others seems closest to Rexroth's organicism; while in Asia, Buddhist philosophy in its ancient tantric manifestation (Nagarjuna, Kūkai, etc.), current contributions of Shingon scholars at Kōya-san and the Zen Kyoto School (which relates Buddhist to Western philosophy through the work of Nishida, Tanabe, Watsuji, Suzuki, Hisamatsu, Nishitani, Takeuchi, Ueda, Abe, and others), and Christian-Buddhist dialogue ranging from that inspired by the late Thomas Merton to ongoing work at Nanzan University in Nagoya, coincides with Rexroth's final outlook. His work also has many fundamental affinities with comparative and anthropological studies of literature, religions, and culture generally, especially with the deep ecology and Buddhist anarchism of Gary Snyder and the Buddhist Peace Fellowship. Such philosophical currents have influenced this study, leading me to conclude that as Buddhism spreads in the West and revives in Asia, Rexroth is sure to be valued as one of its most innovative interpreters. Not in ideas alone, but in sensibility did he find and transmit compassionate wisdom that is rare in the twentieth century, coming to the same conclusion as Kūkai that "Bliss of the Great Void Only is my true Empress."[1]

Whatever their orientation, readers discover an amazing world, many worlds, in Rexroth's work. For rebels and utopians there are furious satires whose targets are perennially with us. But Rexroth's polemics need not alienate readers uncommitted to revolution, for in fact some of his most enduring poems are lyrics of love, nature, and life that appeal to nearly everyone. Perhaps the affirmative side of Rexroth's wisdom is more convincing in the present conservative era than the scorching social protests, which may seem futile. Learning how he created poetry out of despair and ecstacy, disillusionment and realization, we cannot help but live more consciously, compassionately, and creatively in the networks of existence.

Notes

Introduction

1. Outside the United States the most attention to Rexroth's work has come from Japan, probably because of the profound influence of its culture on his poetry, translations, and essays. His work has been translated into Japanese by Yuzuru Katagiri and discussed by Rikutaro Fukuda, Hisao Kanaseki, Sanehide Kodama, Yō Nakayama, Kazuko Shiraishi, Tetsuya Taguchi, and Yorifumi Yaguchi. Rexroth's work has been discussed in Great Britain by Eric Mottram; in Canada by George Woodcock; in France by Yves le Pellec; in Italy by Daniela M. Ciani Forza; and in Hong Kong by Ling Chung.

But in Rexroth's home country he is ignored completely by Helen Vendler in *Part of Nature, Part of Us: Modern American Poets* (Cambridge, Mass.: Harvard University Press, 1980), by Richard Howard in *Alone with America: Essays on the Art of Poetry in the United States since the 1930's* (New York: Atheneum, 1980), and by Jerome Mazzaro, ed., *Modern American Poetry*, (New York: David McKay, 1970). Rexroth is merely quoted on San Francisco poetry in Robert E. Spiller, gen. ed., *A Literary History of the United States* (New York: Macmillan, 1974), pp. 1430–31, 1484; and Rexroth's public readings are briefly mentioned with no discussion of his writings at all in David Perkins, *A History of Modern Poetry from the 1890's to the High Modernist Mode* (Cambridge, Mass.: Harvard University Press, 1976), p. 410. Examples of similar brush-offs could be multiplied.

Without discussing Rexroth's original poetry, Ralph J. Mills quotes Rexroth's criticism in *Contemporary American Poetry*, pp. 26, 89, 179–80, 183, 239, 245, 254, and praises his translations in *Cry of the Human: Essays on Contemporary American Poetry*, pp. 7, 16, 39, 248, 271.

On the other hand, Rexroth is treated fairly as an "iconoclast" in Ihab Hassan, *Contemporary American Literature 1945–1972: An Introduction*, pp. 93–94, 114–19, and with other "west-coast Renascents" in M. L. Rosenthal, *The Modern Poets*, pp. 155–56. Moreover, his personal yet disciplined poems of love and nature are praised in Babette Deutsch, *Poetry in Our Time*, pp. 24–25, 85, 91–92; and the subtlety of his imagery is examined in Joseph Warren Beach, *Obsessive Images: Symbolism in the Poetry of the 1930's and 1940's*, pp. 91, 241, 257–59, 286, 353–59. In addition to commentary in books, dozens of reviews, articles, and essays cover various aspects of his work.

Dissertations by the Chinese poet Ling Chung, Samuel Baity Garren, Linda Hamalian, Rachelle K. Lerner, Emiko Sakurai, and Dorothe Bendon Van Ghent have also advanced the study of Rexroth's work, as have the special issue of *Sagetrieb* 2, no. 3 (Winter, 1983) and the forthcoming *Kenneth Rexroth: Man and Poet* from the University of Maine at Orono, a Festschrift edited by Burton Hatlen and Carroll Terrell.

Donald Hall notes the many reviews and articles listed in my *Kenneth Rexroth* and justly complains that Rexroth has been unfairly slighted by critics, especially those in the academic establishment. "Kenneth Rexroth," *The Weather of Poetry*, pp. 3–11.

2. Ellmann and O'Clair, eds., pp. 14, 699–705.

3. The quotation from Powell appears on the cover of Rexroth's *Excerpts from a Life*. Fiedler, *New York Herald Tribune*, 6 March 1966, p. 10. Carruth, "Our Best Nature Poet," p. 404. Woodcock, "A Rexroth Retrospective," p. 23. Allen Ginsberg and Charles Olsen praised Rexroth in a short, unpublished and undated bio written by Ginsberg and Ted Berrigan for the American Academy of Arts and Letters.

4. Geoffrey Gardner, ed., *For Rexroth* (New York: The Ark 19, 1980), xi, 47, 53, 56, 95.

Rexroth is called "Greatfather of American poetry" by Japan's leading woman poet Kazuko Shiraishi (p. 58); "America's greatest living writer" by Brandeis professor Luis Ellicott Yglesias (p. 110); and "a man of love and learning" with a "voice like gravel down a chute" in a poem by John Ciardi (p. 172).

5. Bly goes on to say that "Snyder's early poems really are mixtures of Rexroth's poems and the Chinese poets, just as my *Silence in the Snowy Fields* is a union of Rexroth and some twentieth century Spanish poets" (*Talking All Morning*, p. 23).

6. Snyder's letter was published in *Kyoto Review* 15 (Fall, 1982): 2. For more on how Snyder was influenced by Rexroth see Bob Steuding, *Gary Snyder*, pp. 19, 22, 45, 110–15, 119–24, 161, 167. Laughlin was interviewed by Robert Dana in *American Poetry Review* (November–December, 1981): 25–26. Rexroth told Brad Morrow that he had recommended to Laughlin publication of Faulkner's *Light in August* and *Sanctuary* and Isherwood's *Berlin Stories* and *All the Conspirators*. "An Interview with Kenneth Rexroth," pp. 48–67. In addition, Rexroth told me that he had urged Laughlin to publish Denise Levertov, Kazuko Shiraishi, Robert Duncan, Jerome Rothenberg, and other poets.

7. Linda Wagner writes: "A new book, *Kenneth Rexroth* (TUSAS 208), is also lively and perceptive. Morgan Gibson gives us some sense of where

Rexroth's aesthetic places him in the wide continuum of modern poetry, emphasizing that for Rexroth the sense of spoken voice, of poem as spoken communication, is primary. Gibson also deals with Rexroth's 'visionary aesthetics,' his stance that the poem has an active responsibility for all mankind's suffering (and joy), and it is this part of Rexroth's belief that led to his involvement in the San Francisco Renaissance, in its early stages." "Poetry: the 1930's to the Present," p. 340. Does she mean that the poet, rather than the poem, is responsible?

Edward Wagenknecht wrote of Rexroth, "It is certainly time for him to have his day in court, and Gibson enters very high claims for him." "4 American Writers."

    8. Daniela M. Ciana Forza, *Poesie di Kenneth Rexroth 1920–1956*, 1982.

Chapter 1   Lives of a Poet: Kenneth Rexroth (1905–1982)

    1. "Martial—XII, LII," *CSP*, p. 164.

    2. "For Eli Jacobson," *CSP*, p. 244.

    3. "On Flower Wreath Hill," *MS*, p. 42.

    4. According to notes on the back cover of *An Autobiographical Novel*, Gilbert Highet predicted that "This book may well become one of the classics of 20th Century autobiography"; according to *Time*, it is "a splendid piece of Americana of a kind that defies academic research"; and according to the *New York Times*, 8 February 1966, p. 2, it "illuminates the texture of an era and portrays the joy of being utterly true to oneself." (See also *New York Times*, 13 February 1966, VIII, p. 5.) James Mark Purcell called the book "a minor American prose classic." "Kenneth Rexroth: Poetics, Populism, and the Chicago Kid," pp. 10–15. On the other hand, Leonard Kriegel griped about Rexroth being "so self-conscious about his emergence as the young artist and Bohemian he becomes the victim of his own life," though he emerges in the book as anything but a victim. "Rexroth: Citizen of Bohemia," p. 688. Leslie Fiedler ridiculed "the world of provincial Bohemia . . . " *New York Herald Tribune*, 6 March 1966, p. 10. But Chicago in the early 1920s, when Rexroth claimed that he had conversed there with D. H. Lawrence, G. K. Chesterton, Sergei Prokoviev, Bertrand Russell, Isadora Duncan, Sherwood Anderson, Carl Sandberg, Frank Lloyd Wright, and other world-famous intellectuals, can hardly be described as provincial. *AN*, p. 130.

    5. *CSP*, pp. 139–42. Rexroth told me that this poem was written to Leslie Smith; but it embodies the kind of ecstacy that he described in *AN* as having experienced also with Andrée and other women.

    6. "Delia Rexroth," *CSP*, p. 186. See another elegy for his mother on p. 153.

    7. *AN*, p. 101. See *Studs Lonigan*, pp. 140–47.

    8. *CSP*, pp. 186, 153. William J. Lockwood has written "Kenneth Rexroth's Chicago Poems."

9. *CLP*, p. 233.

10. *AN*, p. 309. There is a striking resemblance between Rexroth's thought and that of Sapir, who, for example, defined religious sentiment as "a feeling of community with a necessary universe of values." David G. Mandelbaum, ed., *Selected Writings of Edward Sapir* (Berkeley, Calif.: The University of California Press, 1949), p. 356. Sapir also thought that the best poetic style "allows the artist's personality to be felt as a presence, not as an acrobat," because such artists fit "their deeper intuition to the provincial accents of their daily speech" rather than weave "a private, technical art fabric of their own." *Language: An Introduction to the Study of Speech* (New York: Harcourt, Brace & Company, 1921), p. 242.

11. "Climbing Milestone Mountain, August 22, 1937" commemorates the tenth anniversary of Sacco and Vanzetti's execution. *CSP*, pp. 89–90. See also "August 22, 1939," *CSP*, pp. 97–99, and "Fish Peddler and Cobbler," *CSP*, pp. 318–20.

12. Rexroth's first publication was "And now old mammal, gall," *Blues* 1 (June, 1929): 119–20. Other poems, reviews, and essays soon followed in *Morada, Argonaut, Pagany, Poetry, New Review,* and most important, *An "Objectivists" Anthology* (1932), containing his essay on his good friend Yvor Winters, the seven page "Fundamental Disagreement with Two Contemporaries," and "Prolegomena to a Theodicy." In 1949 he produced a revision retitled "A Prolegomenon to a Theodicy" in *The Art of Worldly Wisdom*, dedicating it to Mildred Tokarsky; but since that volume was unsatisfactorily printed, he corrected the poem definitively in the 1953 edition of that collection, and in that form the poem was reprinted in *CLP*, where it is dated 1925–27.

The first publication of his poetry of natural speech, "At Lake Desolation," a poem of revolutionary tragedy, occurred in the *New Republic* on May Day of 1935. In 1937 his publications proliferated to ten poems and three essays, on Marxism, Planners, and Poetry and Society. James Hartzell and Richard Zumwinkle, *Kenneth Rexroth/A Checklist of His Published Writings*, pp. 7–11.

13. There was much confusion about *In What Hour*. Horace Gregory and Marya Zaturenska, welcoming "the arrival of a mature and distinct personality in American literature," praised "regional verse that reflected the charm of the Pacific Coast, and the meditative if somewhat belated contact of a poet with the political and aesthetic 'conversations' of his day." *A History of American Poetry, 1900–1940*, p. 341. Belated? After twenty years of revolutionary thought, writing, and action? "Conversations" hardly conveys Rexroth's commitment to political and artistic movements; and the value of the nature poems is not that they are charmingly regional, but that they set the tragedy of history within creative cycles of nature.

Rolfe Humphries, another condescending critic, appreciated "a simple-minded man with a liking for the outdoors," whose keen observations lead to true lines, but he scolded "the erudite indoor ponderer" who had the foolish idea that abstractions could be "the serviceable material of poetic art." "Too Much Abstraction," p. 221. Such dogmatic rejection of abstraction would, of course, legislate against much important poetry.

More than most critics, Richard Foster understood Rexroth's intellectual and artistic ambitions and achievements, praising especially his "memorable and deeply felt articulations of the special sociological traumata of the thirties," singling out "The Motto on the Sundial" as a kind of "The Second Coming." "The Voice of the Poet: Kenneth Rexroth," p. 380. But Foster did not seem to realize that unlike Yeats's apocalyptic horror of the "rough beast," Rexroth expresses revolutionary hope through the "voice/Preparing to speak," the voice of the oppressed and exploited.

It must be admitted, as William FitzGerald argued, that *In What Hour* is not integrated stylistically, for there are echoes of Eliot, Pound, Stevens, Crane, Auden, and he might have added Aiken and Winters; but he seems not to have heard Rexroth's distinctive voice, sometimes deliberately parodying other poets for the purpose of critically visiting their worlds, a common technique in modern poetry. "Twenty Years at Hard Labor," p. 158.

Other reviews of *In What Hour* appeared in *Christian Century*, 4 September 1940; *Oakland Tribune*, 1 September 1940; *Columbus Dispatch*, 15 September 1940; *Santa Barbara News*, 29 September 1940; *Dallas Times-Herald*, 6 October 1940; *Providence Journal*, 3 November 1940; and *New York Times*, 23 February 1941. The highest praise for the book has come from Robert Hass, who claims that the book seems "to have invented the culture of the West Coast." *Twentieth Century Pleasures: Prose on Poetry*, pp. 223–224.

14. Sanehide Kodama has offered a penetrating analysis of the Japanese influences on the title poem of *The Phoenix and the Tortoise*. *American Poetry and Japanese Culture*, pp. 122–128. Reviewing Rexroth's book, Conrad Aiken wrote: "This is an impressive piece of work, very much alive intellectually, as impressive for its obvious integrity as for its range." *Collected Criticism*, p. 169. August Derleth wrote that the "lines hold to the mind, his images stir before the mind's eye away from the book, his classical allusions are never overdone, he is quotable at almost any line . . . " *Voices* (Winter, 1945). Francis C. Golffing wrote in *Poetry* 65 (February, 1945): 260–62, "Rexroth's poetic endowment is considerable and it is reinforced by a high degree of humanist culture . . . *The Phoenix and the Tortoise* . . . contains passages of great delicacy, precise yet replete with warmth." Vivienne Koch praised "its searching intensity, its rich consciousness of structure in language, and its powerful, almost apocalyptic view of love . . . " *New York Herald Tribune*, 14 January 1945.

15. Responding to my request for an article about the San Francisco Poetry Center for *Arts in Society*, of which I was Poetry Editor, Rexroth wrote me on 15 February 1965:

> Please write to Ruth Witt Diamant and Mark Linenthal for the Poetry Center. I think Ruth is in Japan. For years the Poetry Center was in fact the poetry readings and seminars at my house. When this activity became unmanageable, Robert Duncan, Madeleine

Gleason and I set up the Poetry Center and got Ruth Witt Diamant to sponsor the readings at S. F. State College which was then downtown. Later we got a considerable amount of money from the Rockefeller Foundation and it became a semi-autonomous activity of the college. Today the school has completely absorbed it. Its days as the spearhead of the vanguard are long since gone and the intractables hereabouts refer to it as the antipoetry center. Since local academia is pretty hip, anti-academia is really something, but I suppose they're right. I don't think you should do anything about the Poetry Center without letting Duncan, Ferlinghetti and Brother Antoninus speak their pieces in criticism of it.

16. According to the reprinted 1949 preface to *The Art of Worldly Wisdom*, most of the poems were written from 1927 to 1932, but were not published until "the time which produced them was no longer an element in the judgment of their value." According to the 1953 preface, on the other hand, the poems were written when Rexroth was between seventeen and twenty-one, that is, 1922–27. Still later, in *CSP*, they are dated 1920–30, but the elegy for Andrée could not have been written before her death in 1940.

Gordon K. Grigsby, noting in the volume the "fashionable influences a precocious artist-intellectual was exposed to in those days" from Eliot, Crane, Pound, imagism, etc., speculated that Rexroth must have recognized the immaturity of some of the work, for he had selected only twenty-one lines from the whole book to reprint in *Natural Numbers: New and Selected Poems*, and all of these were from "The Thin Edge of Your Pride." "The Presence of Reality: The Poetry of Kenneth Rexroth," pp. 405–22.

Foster complained that most of the poems in this volume "sounded roughly like a series of grunts, mumblings, and blurtings heard through a motel wall." "The Voice of the Poet: Kenneth Rexroth," pp. 378–80. And even Rexroth's old friend Lawrence Lipton could not agree with him that the cubist poems were "simple, sensuous and passionate," as Rexroth had claimed in the 1949 preface, quoting Milton, though Lipton admired them for inventive playfulness. "The Poetry of Kenneth Rexroth," pp. 168–80.

The strongest praise for *The Art of Worldly Wisdom* came from the classicist Dudley Fitts, who wrote in *Saturday Review*, 17 September 1949, p. 220, "In poem after poem, the reader will find the firm control, the brilliant wit, the quick ear, and the deep humanistic passion that characterizes Mr. Rexroth's mature work.... He is always the convinced, absorbed artist."

17. A few translations from the original edition of *The Signature of All Things* were reprinted in *CSP*. Chinese poems by The Emperor Wu of Han and Tu Mu are reprinted in *Love and the Turning Year: One Hundred More Poems from the Chinese*, pp. 5, 75, and the ones by Tu Fu are reprinted in *One Hundred Poems from the Chinese*, pp. 5, 6, 7, 17, 26, 32. Poems from Greek and Latin are reprinted in *Poems from the Greek Anthology*, pp. 18, 24, 70, 75, 80, 82–87, 90.

Reviewing *Signature*, Richard Eberhart acclaimed "the synthesis of brain and blood," the "slow, controlled, and massive music," "the rock-like foundations of central knowledge and wisdom," the harmony of "cognition and feeling," "the perfection of a form," the "calmness and grandeur" of these poems, "as if something eternal in the natural world has been mastered." *New York Times*, 6 August 1950. Praise also came from Selden Rodman for the nature lyrics ("Gnomic, Fastidious Verses," *New York Herald Tribune*, 7 May 1950); Thomas Hornsby Ferril for the "fastidious architecture" of the poems (*San Francisco Chronicle*, 12 March 1950); from David Ignatow for the "personal utterances" (*New Leader*, 25 March 1950); and from Howard Griffin for the Latin translations (*Saturday Review*, 20 May 1950).

18. Kenneth Rexroth, *Beyond the Mountains* (program notes, New York: The Living Theatre, 1951). "Phaedra: A Dance Play" had originally appeared in *New Directions in Prose and Poetry* 9 (New York: New Directions, 1946), pp. 156–86; "Iphigenia at Aulis" had been published in *Portfolio* 3 (Spring, 1946), Leaf Five, 4 folio pages; and *Beyond the Mountains: A Dance Play* (later called "Hermaios" and not to be confused with the entire tetralogy) had been issued in *Quarterly Review of Literature* 4, no. 3 (1948): 155–92.

William Carlos Williams wrote, "As verse, reading through them, the plays are a delight to me for the very flow of the words themselves. The pith is there, and there with a jolt to it (in the very line, I want to make it clear) that goes well below the surface . . . It is a feat of no mean proportions to raise the colloquial tone to lines of tragic significance . . . I have never been so moved by a play of verse in my time." "Verse with a Jolt to It," p. 5.

The Greek influence on the plays has been judged most authoritatively by George Woodcock, the Canadian critic and classical scholar: "the strange combination of the grandeur that was Greece and the exotic splendour that was Asia which occurs in the two final plays in the volume is, in my experience, unique in modern writing"; and he goes on to admire the "deep philosophic strain running through so much of Rexroth's poetry . . . deriving from combination of the Greek and the Asian . . . ." "Realms beyond the Mountains," pp. 84, 86.

Discussing Japanese influences on Rexroth's plays, Kodama has documented Rexroth's interest in No ever since, as a young man in Chicago, he had acted the part of Cuchullain in his own production of Yeats's *At the Hawk's Well* after consulting Michio Ito, who had danced in Yeats's plays after conferring with him. Rexroth told Kodama in the 1970s that Pound's translations of No, based on Fenollosa's manuscripts, were the best so far; and Rexroth's own plays and essays convinced Kodama of his authoritative understanding of this complex form. Summing up ways in which No had influenced *Beyond the Mountains*, Kodama points to "simple stage setting, a limited number of characters, subtle dramatic responses between the chorus and the characters, concern wtih the past, and allusions to classical literature," as well as "crystallization of emotion by transcendence" in language and dance; and he notes No influences on the direct address and style of

Rexroth's non-dramatic poetry as well. *American Poetry and Japanese Culture*, pp. 128–131. See also his "Kenneth Rexroth and Classical Japanese Poetry," p. 16.

Emiko Sakurai has done the most detailed analyses of No qualities in Rexroth's plays so far, examining the functions of masks, costumes, music, props, setting, dance, the language of characters and chorus, Buddhist themes expressed by the Greek characters, parallels between Yeats's plays and Rexroth's, and ways in which Japanese and Greek influences are fused in Rexroth's plays. "The Oriental Tradition in the Poetry of Kenneth Rexroth," pp. 54–86. See also "The Noh Plays of Kenneth Rexroth: A Study of the Fusion of the Classical Greek and Japanese Traditions," pp. 63–80.

On the other hand, Ruby Cohn doubted the theatrical effectiveness of the plays. "Kenneth Rexroth," pp. 263–65.

19. Reviewing *The Dragon and the Unicorn*, Fitts shrewdly observed that "It is as though in Rexroth we had a Mark Twain who had grown up; who, without yielding an iota of his sense of the absurd and the pitiful, had discarded the clown's motley for the darker dress of the comic philosopher; and who had miraculously been endowed with the power of making poetry." "A Poet Abroad," p. 198.

"This poem says more than it suggests," wrote Richard Eberhart. "It says a good deal... This is poetic art and culture history, with personal evaluation of a fantastic kind, managed with freshness of insight and always some new excitement," "A Voyage of the Spirit," p. 25. Larry Eigner wrote a less enthusiastic appreciation in *Black Mountain Review* (Summer, 1954): 49–57.

Thomas Parkinson called *The Dragon and the Unicorn* "a witness to the love of true righteousness, of mercy, of pity, of love, of knowledge and understanding," concluding that it "seems to be the most perfect artistically of the long meditative poems of the twentieth century." "Kenneth Rexroth, Poet," p. 65. Luis Ellicott Yglesias claimed that "absolutely nothing" during the 1940s "matches it for verbal precision, clarity of intent, and immediacy or depth of perception," preferring it to Lowell's *Lord Weary's Castle*. "Kenneth Rexroth and the Breakthrough into Life," p. 101. And Geoffrey Gardner has written the most thorough interpretation of *The Dragon and the Unicorn* to date: "The Cast Snakeskin and the Uncut Stone," to appear in *Kenneth Rexroth: Man and Poet*.

20. Reviewing *In Defense of the Earth*, R. W. Flint found the poet in "plain statement and lyric celebration, secure in old lives, affections, achievements, and memories." "Poets and Their Subjects," p. 19. Muriel Rukeyser discovered "lyric-mindedness" and "learning that eats the gifts of the world." "Lyrical 'Rage,'" p. 15. M. L. Rosenthal admired some of these poems for their "'savage' relation to truth"; and though he criticized "Thou Shalt Not Kill" for "the self-indulgent pleasure of the poet in love with his own oratory," he nevertheless called Rexroth "the strongest of these West Coast anarchist poets because he is a good deal more than a West Coast

anarchist poet. He is a man of wide cultivation." *The Modern Poets*, pp. 165–66.

21. Henry Miller praised *One Hundred Poems from the Chinese.* "Poems That Grow Like Flowers." Williams called this collection "one of the most brilliantly sensitive books of poems in the American idiom it has been my good fortune to read. . . . As a translator of the Chinese poems of Tu Fu, his ear is finer than anyone I have ever encountered." He also admired *In Defense of the Earth.* "Two New Books by Kenneth Rexroth," pp. 180–90.

22. In *The Dharma Bums*, which Rexroth told me that he had never read because of his antipathy to Jack Kerouac, he was the prototype for Rheinhold Cacoethes, a "bowtied wild-haired old anarchist" who presided over the birth of the Beat generation in 1955 (pp. 11, 13, 152). Contrast Kerouac's sympathetic, though superficial, characterization with Mary McCarthy's sarcastic portrayal of "the poet of the masses," Vincent Keogh, crudely based on Rexroth. *The Groves of Academe*, pp. 272–95. For intimate observations of Rexroth's activities in California from the 1930s into the 1970s, see Janet Richards's *Common Soldiers.* For an informative discussion of Rexroth's relation to the Beats see Brown Miller and Ann Charters, "Kenneth Rexroth," pp. 456–64. See also Yves le Pellec, "Souvenirs de la Baie par Kenneth Rexroth," pp. 155–162; Lee Bartlett, ed., *The Beats: Essays in Criticism*, pp. 1, 2, 4, 43, 134, 149, 187–91, for comments by Thomas Parkinson, William Everson, and Bartlett; and in *Sagetrieb* 2, no. 3 (Winter, 1983), James Broughton, "A Big Bang for Mr. Bangs," pp. 33–36, Thomas Parkinson, "Reflections on Rexroth," pp. 37–44, and Lee Bartlett, "Creating the Autochthon: Kenneth Rexroth, William Everson, and *The Residual Years*," pp. 57–69. Linda Hamalian's interviews with Duncan and Everson concerning Rexroth in San Francisco are also illuminating and are found in *Conjunctions* 4 (1983): 84–96 and *Literary Review* (Spring, 1983): 423–26, respectively. Kodama also discusses Rexroth's role in the San Francisco renaissance. *American Poetry and Japanese Culture*, pp. 131–33.

23. *Quarterly Review of Literature* 9, no. 2 (1957): 1–36. Lipton's introduction, pp. 37–46, establishes the theme of Rexroth's long poems as a "quest for a theodicy," accurately citing such basic influences on *Homestead* as the Arthurian cycle, Frazer's *The Golden Bough*, Breasted's *A History of Egypt*, Proust, Holderin, Apollinaire, Jammes, Rilke, Aiken, and of course Eliot. He shows how "That constant shifting from reverie to narration, from the undersea of the unconscious to geology and archaeology, from inner to outer and back again, was to become Rexroth's outstanding characteristic." Rexroth wrote about the composition of the poem in *AN*, pp. 191–201, 255–58.

Prior to publication of *Homestead* as a whole, two excerpts had appeared in *The Phoenix and the Tortoise*: "Adonis in Winter," beginning "Persephone awaits him" was reprinted in *CSP*, p. 159, and *CLP*, pp. 14–15; and "Adonis in Summer," beginning "The Lotophagi with their silly hands," was reprinted in *CSP*, p. 160, and *CLP*, pp. 13–14.

24. Reviewing *Bird in the Bush*, Alfred Kazin labeled Rexroth an "old-

fashioned American sorehead." "Father Rexroth and the Beats," pp. 54–56. But Foster found much to praise, reading it like "a good novel" by a man of purity, joy, good will, conscience, courage, passion, and intelligence, whose humanism he compared to that of Eliot and the New Critics. "With Great Passion, a Kind of Person," pp. 149–52. Thomas Parkinson praised the essays for Rexroth's "trick of imaginative projections into the life of his subjects. "Phenomenon or Generation?" p. 282.

Foster concluded that Rexroth was a vitally intelligent "original," but was less pleased with *Assays* than with *Bird* and was incensed by "a mad essay called 'The Students Take Over' which announces a nationwide revolution among students on behalf of national and international integrity"—one of Rexroth's predictions that came true. "Lucubrations of an Outside Insider," p. 132.

25. James Laughlin wrote on the cover of the New Directions edition of *Homestead*: "What matters is that a mind sensitive to all the currents of the contemporary situation has put the present and the past together, raised personal experience to an order of values, in a moving and beautiful poem."

26. Alluding to Milton's criteria for poetry, R. V. Cassill stated that in *Natural Numbers* "Rexroth paints a Rexroth as simple, sensuous and passionate as poetry itself is required to be." "Poetic Feast of Simplicity," p. 54.

27. "Venice: May Day," *Natural Numbers,* reprinted in *CSP*, p. 330.

28. Reviewing *CSP*, John Unterecker surveyed Rexroth's development "from egotism to social awareness" and thence to a "more honest . . . still terribly public . . . self-analysis . . . " "Calling the Heart to Order," p. 8.

In a more enthusiastic review of *CSP*, William Stafford showed how the poems "try to tell the truth. Even the determined imagism of many of the poems conveys an air of not wanting to claim more than what *is* . . . " "A Five Book Shelf," p. 188. Stafford understood Rexroth's intention to show in poetry how value resides in fact, as experienced, despite the depersonalizing claims of logical positivists and other intellectuals who isolate facts from values. Or as Fitts put it in an untitled note, "It is not as a kind of latter-day Thersites, the continual complainer of things that are, that Mr. Rexroth will be remembered, but as the loving, wise celebrant of man in his relations with his fellows and with the earth that takes them all." *New York Times*, Section 7, 23 July 1967, p. 8. Grigsby showed how the naturalness of the poems in *CSP* results from self-discipline. "The Presence of Reality," pp. 1–23.

29. *The Heart's Garden* was acclaimed by Richard Eberhart in "Poems of a Japanese Sojourn," Hayden Carruth in *Hudson Review* (Summer, 1968): 404, Emiko Sakurai in "Oriental Tradition," pp. 153–201, 202–208. Luis Ellicott Yglesias, favoring Rexroth over Lowell and other American poets of the 1960s, called *The Heart's Garden* "a perfectly realized meditative poem." "Kenneth Rexroth and the Breakthrough," pp. 96–110.

Also see Kodama's definitive interpretations of *The Heart's Garden* and other poems and plays by Rexroth influenced by Japanese traditions. *American Poetry and Japanese Culture*, pp. 121–53; "Kenneth Rexroth and Classical

Japanese Poetry," pp. 47–52; and "Rexroth and Women," pp. 30–35. *Seiza*, entirely in Japanese, also contains essays on Rexroth by Kodama, Kanaseki, Nakayama, Yaguchi, Katagiri, Gary Snyder, and myself. Yō Nakayama of Kyoto Seika College and Yasuyo Morita have listed much information about Rexroth in relation to Japan in *Kenneth Rexroth Shōshi*, 1984.

30. Samuel Baity Garren has done the most thorough analysis of *CLP* so far in "Quest for Value: A Study of *The Collected Longer Poems* of Kenneth Rexroth," 1976. Reviewing *CLP*, Lawrence Lipton wrote, "Kenneth Rexroth has moved from experience to consolidation . . . He is a major poet of the greatest gifts," *Los Angeles Free Press*, Part II, 10 January 1969, p. 23.

31. After the Buddhist allusions in *Homestead* I do not find any in "Prolegomena to a Theodicy" (written between 1925 and 1927), the short poems of the 1920s collected as *The Art of Worldly Wisdom* (1949), or the short poems of the 1930s in *In What Hour* (1940). From *The Phoenix and the Tortoise* (1944) the influence increases, until by 1967 his outlook is predominantly Buddhist. Concerning Asian influences on Rexroth's work generally, see my "Rexroth's Dharma," pp. 27–37; "Kenneth Rexroth in Japan," pp. 23–28; and "The Buddha-Mind of Kenneth Rexroth," pp. 19–20.

32. *AN*, p. 339.

33. *Excerpts from a Life*, p. 53.

34. He was happy that his students in a "Poetry and Song" workshop "produced several folky rocky numbers, four jazzy-torchy, 4 'art songs' with flute, bass, cello, viola, piano, a bit on the Vaughan Williams Bartok side—but atonal—or polymodal." He ridiculed the typical literary "read-ins" against the war, preferring oral poetry and music in a letter to me of 15 April 1969:

> I can send you tapes of me doing Daniel, & Shadrach Mesach & Abednego to music, and of my workshop singing songs of their own. I strongly urge you to get singers, light shows, rock groups *etc.* and break free of the literary poets—We got from that lady writress at Goucher—Wm Stafford, Allan Brilliant, Galway Kinnell, Robert Bly. Good God! Students want to hear Joni Mitchell, Leonore Kandel, Charles Bukowski, and Country Joe. Uhuru, Kenneth
> . . . Lt. Commander Uhuru in Star Trek—"Michelle"—now *that's* who you need at a Viet Nam read & sing in.

For performances he was trying to find the Industrial Workers of the World *Song Book* and record (letter to me of 4 November 1969): "Did you ever hear Fred Akerstrom, one of Sweden's most popular cafe chantant singers singing the IWW songs in Swedish? a real gas. They become quite respectable poetry in translation, not unlike E. A. Poe."

He asked Laughlin to send New Directions books to war resisters in prison. And he was trying to arrange republication of Matthew Ward's *Indignant Heart*, which I had sent him—described in his first letter to me, in 1957, as "the only convincing story of a proletarian Negro I have ever read—

it sounds like it was written by a worker—not a novelist." Written by a Detroit auto worker who had become a colleague of Raya Dunayevskaya, formerly one of Trotsky's secretaries in Mexico, the autobiography was eventually reprinted. Charles Denby (Matthew Ward), *Indignant Heart: A Black Worker's Journal* (Boston: South End Press, 1978).

35. Denouncing both Nixon and Humphrey, Rexroth had written me on 21 July 1968:

> If it's Tweedledick and Tweedlehump this Fall, people are going to flood out of the country. In California it will certainly be Max Raferty. *No* nation on earth has 3 top politicians like Rafferty, Reagan, Murphy. And do you realize that Wallace will get *twice* the percentage of vote of the W. German 'Neo Nazis' who are far less reactionary?

"The Anti-Vietnam forces won't print me," he wrote on 3 August. "I've gone down the memory hole." But even if militants thought of him as "out of it," the steady stream of his books advanced the cultural revolution.

36. He said of a draft of *Kenneth Rexroth*: "It does seem to me to portray me primarily as an anarchist and give less emphasis to the religious and nature mysticism and to the erotic mysticism." But after sending me some corrections and receiving the published book in 1972 he exclaimed, "Gibson on Rexroth just came & is *great*—very conscientious & very complimentary. I am deeply grateful." (Undated letters to me.)

37. Kodama praised the Japanese translations in "Rexroth and Women," pp. 30–35. Rikutaro Fukuda found them "brusk," *In the Shade of the West: Essays on Comparative Literature*, pp. 158–59.

38. Discussing *New Poems*, Leslie B. Mittleman preferred Rexroth's translations to his original poems. *Masterplots*, Frank N. McGill, ed., pp. 209–11.

39. See Ling Chung, "Kenneth Rexroth and Chinese Poetry: Translation, Imitation, and Adaptation," 1972. Elsewhere she reports, "How fast and directly could he grasp the pathos of a Chinese poet! How in the most accurate and unexpected ways could he transform and recreate an image from the Chinese poetic language into English." "Forty Years in Between," pp. 11–13. Also, William J. Lockwood has written "Kenneth Rexroth's Versions of Li Ch'ing Chao."

40. Concerning Rexroth's career as a painter, see Beatrice Farwell, "Kenneth Rexroth: Life at the Cultural Frontier," *Gallery Notes*, with reproductions of some of his paintings and a cover photograph of Rexroth by myself. Farwell was Guest Curator of the Rexroth exhibition at the Santa Barbara Museum of Art and Professor of Art History at the University of California, Santa Barbara. Rachelle K. Lerner is currently writing a dissertation at the University of Toronto on Rexroth's painting in relation to his poetry, with especial attention to his theory of cubism.

41. I am indebted to Carol Tinker for information about the funeral in her letter to me of 17 May 1984, and to Father Huerta for information about

the Roman Catholic baptism and for permission to quote from his unpublished eulogy, "*In What Hour.*"

Allen Ginsberg wrote an obituary of Rexroth, with the help of Ted Berrigan, but it has not been published. See my "Tribute," pp. 179–82; my obituary in *Poetry Flash* 113 (August, 1982): 8; and Jean W. Ross's interview of me in *Contemporary Authors New Revision Series* 14 (Detroit: Gale, 1985): 400–403. According to Eliot Weinberger, his own obituary first requested by *The Nation* was then rejected there by an editor who ruled out Rexroth as a "minor writer" and "sexist pig," although the journal had published Rexroth's work ever since the 1930s and he had promoted countless women poets. Weinberger's obituary was published as "Kenneth Rexroth 1905–1982" in *Sulfur* 5 (1982): 4–6. Weinberger reported on some editors' antipathies to Rexroth in "At the Death of Kenneth Rexroth," pp. 45–53.

42. *Kenneth Rexroth yaku, Marichiko no Ai no Uta, Katagiri Yuzuru ni yoru Fukugen no kokoromi* (The Love Poems of Marichiko, translated by Kenneth Rexroth—An Attempt at Restoration by Yuzuru Katagiri.) Here Katagiri honors Rexroth's myth of the poems' origin.

Kenneth Rexroth Hanawa no Oka nite, sonota no Nihon de kakareta Shi, 1974–75, Katagiri Yuzuru yaku (Kenneth Rexroth, On Flower Wreath Hill and other Poems Written in Japan, 1974–75, translated by Yuzuru Katagiri). Including *The Silver Swan.*

Kenneth Rexroth, Kokoro no Niwa, Hanawa no Oka nite, sonota no Nihon no Shi, Katagiri Yuzuru yaku (Kenneth Rexroth, The Heart's Garden, On Flower Wreath Hill, and Other Poetry of Japan, translated by Yuzuru Katagiri), including *The Silver Swan* and my "Kaisetsu" (Comment) on Rexroth's Buddhism, also translated by Katagiri, pp. 96–102.

Because of the great influence of Kūkai and Shingon Buddhism on Rexroth's poetry and thought, he had urged Hiroshi Murakami and me to publish our English version of Kūkai's poetry, with commentaries, first in *Zero* (Fall, 1979): 176–188, and then in *Tantric Poetry of Kūkai (Kōbō Daishi) Japan's Buddhist Saint,* edited by Professor Montri Umavijani (Bangkok, Thailand: Mahachulalonghorn Buddhist University, 1982).

43. "Kenneth Rexroth's Epiphany: June 6, 1982," p. 16.

44. A few of the reviews of *Selected Poems* published so far are: Tom Clark, "Natural Wonders"; James Hazard, "A Thin Valuable Look at Rexroth's Poetry"; Marjorie Perloff, "Poetry and the Common Life," pp. 160–64; and my own in *American Poetry* 3, no. 2 (Winter, 1986): 86–89.

Chapter 2   "*Poetry Is Vision*"—"*Vision Is Love*": Rexroth's Philosophy of Literature

1. "The Surprising Journey of Father Lonergan," *The Elastic Retort,* p. 274.

2. "Poetry, Regeneration, and D. H. Lawrence," *Bird in the Bush,* p. 18. Reprinted from *Selected Poems of D. H. Lawrence.*

3. *CLP*, p. 285.

4. *CSP*, p. 48.

5. *The Heart's Garden, The Garden's Heart*, *CLP*, p. 285.

6. *CLP*, p. 295.

7. "About the Poems," *The Phoenix and the Tortoise* (1944), p. 10. Albert Schweitzer illustrates Rexroth's concept of the realized "true person."

8. "Berenike," *BM*, p. 181.

9. Introduction to *CLP*, n. p. See also: "The 'holy' is not the Judaeo-Protestant 'utterly other'—a term of Otto's—but the utterly same." "American Indian Songs," *Assays*, p. 58.

10. *AN*, p. 152.

11. *MS*, p. 20.

12. *The Phoenix and the Tortoise*, p. 90.

13. *American Poetry in the Twentieth Century*, p. 52.

14. *Bird in the Bush*, pp. 5, 12.

15. Ibid., p. 5.

16. Ibid., p. 5.

17. Ibid., p. 16.

18. Ibid., p. 7.

19. "Poetry, Regeneration, and D. H. Lawrence," *Bird in the Bush*, p. 193.

20. *CSP*, p. 227.

21. Preface to *The Signature of All Things*, p. 10.

22. *AN*, pp. 192, 256–58.

23. *CLP*, p. 14, reprinted in a passage entitled "Adonis in Summer," *CSP*, p. 160.

24. Jerome Rothenberg, ed., *The Revolution of the Word: A New Gathering of American Avant Garde Poetry, 1914–1945* (New York: Continuum, 1974).

25. *AN*, pp. 149–50.

26. Introduction to *The New British Poets: An Anthology*, p. ix. See also *American Poetry in the Twentieth Century*, p. 100 and *passim*.

27. *CSP*, p. 27.

28. 1949 Preface to *The Art of Worldly Wisdom*, reprinted in the 1953 edition, n. p.

29. Preface to *Pierre Reverdy Selected Poems*, pp. vi–vii.

30. *CSP*, p. 5. Comparing Rexroth's cubism with the work of Gertrude Stein and Laura Riding, Dorothe Bendon Van Ghent showed how images are abstracted from personal experience so they are dissociated—"just as Alice saw the smile of the Cheshire cat hanging lone and unattended, abstracted from the cat." Towards such objects, she argued, the reader can observe language in a process of emergence, like things of nature, and is left free to have his own attitudes and feelings, whereas traditional poetry controls the reader's experience. She concluded her perceptive interpretation by comparing Rexroth with Dante in moral and intellectual commitments. "Some Problems of Communication," pp. 1–15.

But there are problems with Rexroth's cubism which cannot be solved in the present study. In a letter to me of 11 December 1982, Marjorie Perloff wondered how cubist Rexroth's work really is: "I know he thought of himself that way but to me the Andromeda poem you cite seems very different—perhaps more Surrealist than Cubist. There are fragmented images but as you say, one experiences extreme vertigo—and it's something of a visionary poem whereas Cubist work usually deals with fragmented images from a single discourse radius, faceted, made ambiguous. The Rexroth poem is not ambiguous in that sense, is it? In other words, if you take Gombrich's definition of Cubism as the art form in which images cancel each other out, in which it's impossible to apply the test of consistency, then I don't really feel this is a model. Cubism was also opposed to mysticism." These are shrewd observations. I find the poem more ambiguously fragmented than she does; but if she is right that Rexroth's practice did not conform to Cubist theory, that may have been an important motive for his turning to "natural numbers" and excelling in that mode.

31. *Pierre Reverdy*, p. x.

32. This translation begins, "When We with Sappho," *CSP*, p. 139, and *AN*, p. 154. A shortened poem is in *Poems from the Greek Anthology*, p. 90.

33. *CSP*, pp. 34–35.

34. *CSP*, pp. 234–36, 180–81, 101–4, respectively.

35. *AN*, p. x.

36. "Unacknowledged Legislators," *Bird in the Bush*, pp. 16, 5.

37. W. C. Williams, *The Collected Later Poems* (New York: New Directions, 1963), p. 13.

38. Rexroth reviewed Buber's *I and Thou* (New York: Scribner, 1958) in "The Hasidism of Martin Buber," *Bird in the Bush*, pp. 106–42, and frequently alluded to his ideas in conversation and writing.

39. "Preface" to the 1802 edition of *Lyrical Ballads*, ed. H. Littledale (London: Oxford, 1911), p. 237.

40. *Assays*, p. 57.

41. *AN*, p. 252.

42. *AN*, pp. 19, 67–79, 91, 114, 332–39, for example.

43. *CSP*, pp. 237–43, 260–65, 255, respectively.

44. *CSP*, pp. 153, 186, 154, 166, 190 respectively.

45. *MS*, pp. 47–82.

46. *CLP*, pp. 123, 128, 140, and *passim*.

47. *The Phoenix and the Tortoise*, p. 9.

48. *CSP*, pp. 193–95. See also "A Public Letter for William Carlos Williams' Seventy-Fifth Birthday," *Assays*, pp. 202–5, and *American Poetry in the Twentieth Century*, pp. 75–84 and *passim*. A longer interpretation of the poem is contained in my *Kenneth Rexroth*, pp. 17–20.

Chapter 3   The Poems

1. Contrasting Pound's "When the nightingale to his mate" to Rexroth's "When the nightingale cries," Thomas Parkinson has brilliantly

shown how the older translation calls attention to its own artistry, whereas Rexroth focused on love *through* the words of the poem, as if wisdom were more important than art as an end in itself. "Kenneth Rexroth, Poet," pp. 56–57.

2. *Selected Poems of D. H. Lawrence*, p. 70.

3. Jacob Boehme, *The Signature of All Things* (London: J. M. Dent & Sons, 1934), p. 91.

4. Quoted by Evelyn Underhill in *Mysticism* (New York: Dutton, 1961), p. 58.

5. Quoted by Sidney Spenser, *Mysticism in World Religion* (Baltimore, Md., 1961), p. 269.

6. The theme, form, and refrain of "Thou Shalt Not Kill" were adapted from "Lament of the Makeris" by the Scot Dunbar, who wrote

> hes done petuously devour
> The noble Chaucer, of makeris flowr,
> The Monk of Bery, and Gower, all thre:
> Timor mortis conturbat me . . .

The Poems of William Dunbar, edited by W. Mackay MacKenzie (Edinburgh: The Porpoise Press, 1932), p. 21.

7. W. C. Williams wrote that "Thou Shalt Not Kill" should be displayed in all universities, in "Two New Books by Kenneth Rexroth," p. 183.

8. *Assays*, pp. 151–52.

9. The prosody of "Prolegomena" and other poems is discussed by Lipton, "The Poetry of Kenneth Rexroth," pp. 168–80, and Van Ghent, "Some Problems of Communication," pp. 73, 95, and *passim*. For comparisons with preliterate chants, see C. M. Bowra, *Primitive Song* (New York: World, 1962), pp. 63–88.

10. Kintsune's poem is included also in *One Hundred Poems from the Japanese*, p. 42.

11. *Excerpts from a Life*, p. 32.

12. Kenneth K. S. Ch'en, *Buddhism: the Light of Asia* (Woodbury, New York: Barron's Educational Series, 1968), pp. 160–61. The original Indian sutra of 400,000 lines is no longer extant as a whole, but Thomas Cleary has translated some of the extant portion from Chinese as *The Flower Ornament Scripture* (Boulder, Colo.: Shambala, 1984) vol. 1.

13. According to Kang-Nam Oh, in the relativistic and organic philosophy of the *Flower Wreath Sutra* reality is a process of "interfusion and dissolution, co-existence and annihilation, adversity and harmony." "Dharmadhattu—An Introduction to Hua-yen Buddhism," *The Eastern Buddhist* 12, no. 2 (October, 1979): 72–91. For a Zen interpretation of the Flower Wreath philosophy, see Christmas Humphries, *Buddhism* (Harmondsworth, England: Penguin), pp. 150–51.

14. Yoshito S. Hakeda, *Kūkai: Major Works* (New York: Columbia University Press, 1972), p. 213. For a poetic expression of these ideas and images see Gibson and Murakami, *Tantric Poetry of Kūkai*.

15. The Flower Wreath cosmology is compared with Leibniz's monadology in Masaharu Anesaki, *History of Japanese Buddhism* (Rutland, Vt.: Tuttle, 1963), p. 94. Leibniz's influence on Rexroth is shown in his poem "Monads." *CSP*, p. 176.

16. Kodama has briefly compared Rexroth's Japanese allusions in *The Phoenix and the Tortoise* to Pound's method of superposition of images and Eliot's method of reflecting Dante's *Divina Comedia* in *The Waste Land. American Poetry and Japanese Culture*, pp. 122–28; "Kenneth Rexroth and Classical Japanese Poetry," pp. 8–13. For my comments on Kodama's work see my review of *American Poetry and Japanese Culture* in *Comparative Literature Studies* (Spring, 1986) and in "Rexroth's Dharma," pp. 29–30.

17. In the preface to the 1952 edition of *The Dragon and the Unicorn* Rexroth made comparisons with travel writings by Mark Twain and by Clough and Rogers. See "Amours de Voyages," written in 1849, in *The Poems of Arthur Hugh Clough*, H. F. Lawry, A. L. P. Norrington, and F. L. Milhauser, eds. (Oxford: Oxford University Press, 1951), pp. 177–220, and Samuel Rogers's "Italy," *Poetic Works* (Philadelphia, Penn., 1966), pp. 221–451.

18. *One Hundred More Poems from the Japanese* (1974), p. 9. Other translations of Akiko and notes about her appear on pp. 5–20 and 110–11 of that volume and in *The Burning Heart: Women Poets of Japan* (translations by Rexroth in collaboration with Ikuko Atsumi), pp. 63–66, 87, 149–50. These translations, her life, and her work, are examined by Keiko Matsui Gibson and myself in "Yosano Akiko," pp. 1713–19.

19. In 1976 five of the Marichiko poems had originally appeared in *One Hundred More Poems from the Japanese*, pp. 37–41, with Romaji versions by himself and Yasuyo Morita, and with a note that "MARICHIKO is the pen name of a contemporary young woman who lives near the temple of Marishi-ben in Kyoto," p. 114. Variants of four of these poems were printed with eight others as "Translations from the Japanese of Marichiko" in *New Poems*, pp. 37–42. Not reprinted in *The Morning Star* was the first poem of the 1978 edition of *Marichiko*, "Full Moon." The Watershed Foundation (Washington, D. C.) has issued a tape recording of Rexroth reading some of the Marichiko poems with Akiko's poems in Japanese and English, with Japanese music. See Kodama on the later poems in *American Poetry and Japanese Culture*, pp. 144–53.

Chapter 4   The Plays: Beyond the Mountains (1951)

1. Preface to *The Signature of All Things*, p. 9. Yeats's description of No as a nonnaturalistic drama in which masked players move and dance like puppets and sing as well as speak applies to Rexroth's plays. William Butler Yeats, "Certain Noble Plays of Japan," *Essays and Introductions* (London: Macmillan, 1961), p. 250.

2. Menander, who lived about 125–95 B.C., is called Melinda in the

popular Pali dialogues, *Questions of King Melinda*, parts of which are translated in Lucien Stryk, ed., *World of the Buddha* (Garden City , N. Y.: Anchor Books, Doubleday, 1969), pp. 89–142. Throughout this study I have not tried to cite sources for commonly known Buddhist ideas. Stryk's anthology is an excellent introduction for readers of Rexroth who are unfamiliar with basic Buddhist texts.

3. Arthur Waley, introduction, *The Noh Plays of Japan* (New York: Grove Press, n. d.), p. 21.

4. Rexroth, *Classics Revisited*, p. 59.

5. David Grene and Richmond Lattimore, eds. and trans., Introduction to "Hippolytus," *Euripides* 1 (New York: Modern Library, 1967), p. 167. See also H.D.F. Kitto, *Greek Tragedy* (Garden City, N. Y.: Penguin, 1954), p. 213.

6. Charles R. Walker, trans., *Iphigenia at Aulis*, in *The Complete Greek Tragedies*, Vol. 4: *Euripides* (University of Chicago Press, 1959), pp. 361, 370.

7. *The Collected Plays of William Butler Yeats* (New York: Macmillan, 1953), p. 364.

8. Ibid.

Chapter 5   Translation as an "Act of Sympathy"

1. "The Poet As Translator," *Assays*, pp. 19, 39.

Chapter 6   Rexroth as Culture-Critic

1. *Tantric Poetry of Kūkai*, p. 25.

Bibliography

For annotations, see the bibliography compiled by Morgan Gibson and Burton Hatlen, eds. in *Kenneth Rexroth: Man and Poet*, (University of Maine at Orono Press, forthcoming.)
See also James Hartzell and Richard Zumwinkle, *Kenneth Rexroth/a Checklist of His Published Writings*, with a foreword by Lawrence Clark Powell (Los Angeles: Friends of the University of California at Los Angeles Library, 1967).
A bibliography of items for and about Rexroth in Japan (in Japanese) is Yō Nakayama and Yasuyo Morita, *Kenneth Rexroth Shoshi* (Kyoto: Kenneth Rexroth Poetry Award Committee, c/o Kyoto Seika College, 1984).
Japanese items below have been translated by Keiko Matsui Gibson.

By Rexroth

Autobiographies

"A Crystal Out of Time and Space: The Poet's Diary." *Conjunctions* 8 (1985): 62–80.
An Autobiographical Novel (AN). Garden City, N. Y.: Doubleday, 1966. Reprint Weybridge, England: Whittet, 1977. Reprint Santa Barbara, Calif.: Ross-Erikson, 1978.
Excerpts from a Life. Foreword by Ekbert Fass. Santa Barbara, Calif.: Conjunctions, 1981. Passages reprinted in *Conjunctions* 4 (1983): 96–114 and in *Sagetrieb* 2, no. 3 (Winter, 1983): 9–17.

Verse Plays

Beyond the Mountains (BM). New York: New Directions, 1951. Reprint San Francisco: City Lights, n. d. Reprint London: Routledge, 1951. Preface and *Phaedra, Iphigenia, Hermaios,* and *Berenike.*

See also program notes entitled *The Living Theatre*. Kenneth Rexroth. *Beyond the Mountains*. New York: The Living Theatre, 1951. Copy in the Lilly Library, Indiana University.

Poetry

In What Hour. New York: Macmillan, 1940.

The Phoenix and the Tortoise. New York: New Directions, 1944.

The Art of Worldly Wisdom. Prairie City, Ill.: Decker Press, 1949. Reprint Sausalito, Calif.: Golden Goose Press, 1953 and 1973. Reprint Santa Barbara, Calif.: Morrow and Covici, 1980.

The Signature of All Things. New York: New Directions, 1950.

The Dragon and the Unicorn. Norfolk, Conn.: New Directions, 1952.

A Bestiary for My Daughters Mary and Katherine. San Francisco: Bern Porter, 1955.

Thou Shalt Not Kill: A Memorial for Dylan Thomas. Sunnyvale, Calif.: Horace Schwartz, A Goad Publication, 1955.

In Defense of the Earth. New York: New Directions, 1956. Reprint London: Hutchinson, 1959.

Six Poems. New York: New Directions, 1957.

The Homestead Called Damascus. World Poets Series, New York: New Directions, 1963.

Natural Numbers: New and Selected Poems. New York: New Directions, 1963.

The Collected Shorter Poems (CSP). New York: New Directions, 1966. Reprint 1967 and 1976.

The Heart's Garden, The Garden's Heart. Cambridge, Mass.: Pym-Randall Press, 1967.

Penguin Modern Poets 9: Denise Levertov, Kenneth Rexroth, William Carlos Williams, pp. 45–73. Harmondsworth, Middlesex, England: Penguin Books, 1967.

The Spark in the Tinder of Knowing. Cambridge, Mass.: Pym-Randall Press, 1968.

The Collected Longer Poems (CLP). New York: New Directions, 1968. Reprint 1970.

Sky Sea Birds Trees Earth House Beasts Flowers. Santa Barbara, Calif.: Unicorn Press, 1971. Reprint 1973.

The Kenneth Rexroth Reader. Eric Mottram, ed. London: Cape, 1972.

New Poems (NP). New York: New Directions, 1974.

The Silver Swan. Port Townsend, Wash.: Copper Canyon Press, 1976.

On Flower Wreath Hill. Burnaby, British Columbia: Blackfish Press, 1976.

The Love Poems of Marichiko. Santa Barbara, Calif.: Christopher's Books, 1978.

The Morning Star (MS). New York: New Directions, 1979. Containing *The Silver Swan, On Flower Wreath Hill,* and *The Love Poems of Marichiko.*

Saucy Limericks and Christmas Cheer. Santa Barbara, Calif.: Bradford Morrow, 1980.

Between Two Wars. Fourteen Poems from *In What Hour.* Introduction by Bradford Morrow. Interview with Rexroth conducted by Daniel Goldstein. Edited, designed, and printed by Richard Bigus. Athens, Ohio: Labyrinth Editions, and San Francisco: Iris Press, 1982.

Selected Poems. Edited with an introduction by Bradford Morrow. New York: New Directions, 1984.

Japanese Translations of Rexroth's Poetry

Kenneth Rexroth yaku, Marichiko no Ai no Uta, Katagiri Yuzuru ni yoru Fukugen no Kokoromi (The Love Poems of Marichiko, translated by Kenneth Rexroth—an Attempt at Restoration by Yuzuru Katagiri). Kyoto: Kawaraban, 1978. The poems are actually not translations by Rexroth, but his original work.

Kenneth Rexroth Hanawa no Oka nite, sonota no Nihon de kakareta Shi, 1974–75, Katagiri Yuzuru yaku (Kenneth Rexroth, On Flower Wreath Hill and other Poems Written in Japan, 1974–75, translated by Yuzuru Katagiri). Including *The Silver Swan.* Kyoto: Kawaraban, Kyoto Seika Tankidaigaku, 1979.

Kenneth Rexroth, Kokoro no Niwa, Hanawa no Oka nite, sonota no Nihon no Shi, Katagiri Yuzuru yaku (Kenneth Rexroth, The Heart's Garden, On Flower Wreath Hill, and Other Poetry of Japan, translated by Yuzuru Katagiri). Ikayama: Techosha,

1984. Including "Kaisetsu" (Comment) by Morgan Gibson, pp. 95–102.

Rexroth's Translations of Poetry

From Spanish:

Thirty Spanish Poems of Love and Exile. San Francisco: City Lights Pocket Bookshop, 1956.

From French:

Fourteen Poems by O. V. de L. Milosz. San Francisco: Peregrine Press, 1952. Reprint Seattle: Copper Canyon Press, 1982.
One Hundred Poems from the French. Highlands, N. C.: Jargon Society, 1955. Cambridge, Mass.: Pym-Randall, 1972.
Pierre Reverdy Selected Poems. New York: New Directions, 1969. Reprint London: Cape, 1973.

From Greek and Latin:

Poems from the Greek Anthology. Ann Arbor: University of Michigan Press, 1962.

From Japanese:

One Hundred Poems from the Japanese (PJ). New York: New Directions, 1955. Reprint, 1957 and 1964.
One Hundred More Poems from the Japanese (More PJ). New York: New Directions, 1974. Reprint 1976.
The Burning Heart: Women Poets of Japan. With Ikuko Atsumi. New York: A Continuum Book, Seabury Press, 1977.
Seasons of Sacred Lust: Selected Poems of Kazuko Shiraishi. With Carol Tinker, Ikuko Atsumi, John Solt, and Yasuyo Morita. New York: New Directions, 1978.

From Chinese:

One Hundred Poems from the Chinese (PC). New York: New Directions, 1956. Reprint 1965 and 1970.
Love in the Turning Year: One Hundred More Poems from the Chinese. New York: New Directions, 1970.
The Orchid Boat: Women Poets of China. With Ling Chung. New York: Herder and Herder, McGraw Hill, 1972.

Li Ch'ing Chao: Complete Poems. With Ling Chung. New York: New Directions, 1979.

Essays

Bird in the Bush: Obvious Essays (BB). New York: New Directions, 1959. Reprint 1979. Arno Reprint, 1959.
Assays. New York: New Directions, 1961.
Classics Revisited. Chicago: Quadrangle Books, 1968.
The Alternative Society: Essays from the Other World. New York: An Azimuth Book, Herder and Herder, 1970. Reprint 1974.
With Eye and Ear. New York: An Azimuth Book, Herder and Herder, 1970. Reprint 1974.
American Poetry in the Twentieth Century. New York: Herder and Herder, 1971. Reprint New York: A Continuum Book, Seabury Press, 1973.
The Elastic Retort: Essays in Literature and Ideas. New York: A Continuum Book, Seabury Press, 1973.
Communalism: Its Origins to the Twentieth Century. New York: A Continuum Book, Seabury Press, 1974.

Uncollected Prose

Rexroth's Introductions to his volumes of poetry and translations.
"The Function of the Poet in Society." Undated; pre-1940 because of typescript poems from *In What Hour*; one of the most important unpublished items in the Rexroth collection, University of California at Los Angeles.
"Literature." *The Encyclopaedia Brittanica* 15th Edition, pp. 1041–50. Chicago: Brittanica, 1974.
"Vivienne Renaud." *Conjunctions* 2 (Summer, 1982): 54–59. Story.
"The Commercialization of the Image of Revolt." Ann Charters, ed. *The Beats: Literary Bohemians in Postwar America. Dictionary of Literary Biography.* Vol. 2, pp. 643–50. Detroit: Gale, 1983.

Rexroth's Introductions in his editions of:

Selected Poems of D. H. Lawrence. New York: New Directions, 1947. New York: Viking/Compass, 1961. Reprint 1968.
The New British Poets: An Anthology. New York: New Directions, 1949.
Ford, Ford Madox. *Buckshee.* Edited, with introductions, by Rex-

roth and Robert Lowell. Cambridge, Mass.: Pym-Randall, 1964.

Berkman, Alexander. *Prison Memoirs of an Anarchist*. Pittsburgh: Frontier Press, 1970.

Meltzer, David. *Tens: Selected Poems 1961–1971*. New York: A Continuum Book, McGraw Hill, 1973.

Milosz, Czeslaw. *Selected Poems*. Translations mostly by others. New York: A Continuum Book, Seabury Press, 1973.

Hagedorn, Jessica Tarahata, Alice Karle, Barbara Szerlip, and Carol Tinker. *Four Young Women: Poems*. New York: A Continuum Book, McGraw Hill, 1973.

Mallory, Lee. *20 Times in the Same Place: An Anthology of Santa Barbara Poetry*. Carpenteria, Calif.: Painted Cave Books, 1973.

Aridjis, Homero. *Blue Spaces: Selected Poems*. New York: A Continuum Book, Seabury Press, 1974.

The Buddhist Writings of Lafcadio Hearn. Santa Barbara, Calif.: Ross-Erikson, 1977.

G. R. S. Mead, ed. *Fragments of a Faith Forgotten: The Gnostics, etc.* New Hyde Park, N. Y.: University Books, 1960.

Tolstoy, Leon. *The Kingdom of God Is Within You*. New York: Noonday, 1961.

Everson, William. *The Residual Years: Poems, 1934–1948*. New York: New Directions, 1968.

Halpert, Stephen. *A Return to Pagany: The History, Correspondence, and Selections from a Little Magazine*. Boston: Beacon Press, 1969.

Read, Sir Herbert. *The Green Child*. New York: New Directions, n. d.

Interviews

Bridson, D. G. "A Conversation with Kenneth Rexroth." Washington, D. C., Broadcast from London on the B. B. C. Third Programme, 10 June 1963. Unpublished text in the Lilly Library, Indiana University.

Ossman, David, ed. "Kenneth Rexroth," *The Sullen Art*, pp. 10–16. New York: Corinth Books, 1963.

"Kenneth Rexroth." *Quixote* 3, no. 4 (Spring, 1968): 85–86. This interview was so garbled that Rexroth repudiated it.

Pondrom, Cyrena N. "Interview with Kenneth Rexroth." At the University of Wisconsin at Madison, 23 March 1968, and Milwaukee, 24 March 1968. *Contemporary Literature* 10, no. 3 (Summer, 1969): 313–31. Reprinted in L. S. Denbo and Cyrena N. Pondrom, eds. *The Contemporary Writer: Interviews with Sixteen Writers and Poets.* Madison: University of Wisconsin Press, 1972.

Meltzer, David, ed. "Kenneth Rexroth." *The San Francisco Poets*, pp. 9–55. New York: Ballantine, 1971.

"An Interview with Kenneth Rexroth." *PHP* (Tokyo, October, 1973): 33–39

McKenzie, James J., and Robert W. Lewis, eds. "That Rexroth— He'll Argue You into Anything: An Interview with Kenneth Rexroth." *North Dakota Quarterly* 44, no. 3 (1976): 7–33.

Lerner, Eric, ed. "The Jewel Net of Indra." *Zero: Contemporary Buddhist Life and Thought* 2 (1979): 26–40.

Morrow, Bradford, ed. "An Interview with Kenneth Rexroth." *Conjunctions* 1 (Festschrift in honor of James Laughlin, 1981): 48–67.

Ferris, Lester. *Between Two Wars.* Athens, Ohio: Labyrinth Editions, and San Francisco: Iris Press, 1982.

Katagiri, Yuzuru, ed. and trans. (Japanese). "Kenneth Rexroth at Hon Yara Do, January 15, 1975." *Kino-Hyoron* (Kino Review) 14 (March, 1983): 92–110.

Recordings

San Francicso Poets. New York: Evergreen Records 1, n. d.

Poetry Readings in "The Cellar." San Francisco: Fantasy Records 7002, 1957.

Kenneth Rexroth at the Black Hawk. San Francisco: Fantasy Records 7008, 1960. *Treasury of 100 Modern American Poets* 9. New York: Spoken Arts, n. d. Record.

A Sword in a Cloud of Light. Washington, D. C.: The Watershed Foundation, 1977. Tape.

Unpublished Papers

Letters from Kenneth Rexroth to Morgan Gibson, 1957–1979. Owned by Gibson, who is editing them for publication as a collection.

Other papers are in Rexroth collections at the University of California, Los Angeles, and the University of Southern California.

On Rexroth

Collections

Gardner, Geoffrey, ed. *For Rexroth*. Festschrift. New York: *The Ark* 19, 1980. Festschrift containing prose by Gardner, Andreae, Bruchac, Chung, Ciani, Everson, M. Gibson, Gidlow, Haines, Kirsch, Kodama, Lawler, Meltzer, Merwin, Morrow, Sakurai, Shiraishi, Woodcock, Wright, and Yglesias (each listed below with titles); poetry and some fiction by Carol Tinker and eighty-four other writers from Asia, Europe, and the Americas; six drawings by Morris Graves; and "Chidori" by Rexroth.

Jenkins, Joyce, ed. *Poetry Flash* 113 (August, 1982). Memorial prose and poetry by Jenkins, Meltzer, M. Gibson, McClure, Dery, Parkinson, Ferlinghetti, Safdie, and Antler. With photographs.

Katagiri, Yuzuru, ed. *Kenneth Rexroth 1905–82*. Kyoto: Rexroth Poetry Award Committee, Kyoto Seika College, 1982. Memorials in poetry and prose, mostly in Japanese.

Jennison, Rebecca, Yuzuru Katagiri, and Edith Shiffert, eds. *Kyoto Review* 15 (Kyoto, Japan, Fall, 1982). Rexroth Memorial Issue. Prose by Snyder, Kodama, and M. Gibson; poetry by Akiyama, Solt, Shiraishi, Shiffert, Antler, Hunt, and Katagiri; all in English; with photographs.

Seiza: Kenneth Rexroth Tokushu (Tokyo: Takeo Yatate, Fall, 1982). Rexroth Memorial Issue (in Japanese). Prose by Kodama, Kanaseki, Nakayama, Yaguchi, Katagiri, Snyder, and M. Gibson (translated by Keiko Matsui Gibson).

Hatlen, Burton, and Carroll F. Terrell, eds. *Sagetrieb: Special Issue Kenneth Rexroth* 2, no. 3 (Winter, 1983). University of Maine at Orono. Rexroth, "Three Excerpts from a Life"; poems by Tinker, Hamill, Morrow, McClure, Tarn; prose by Robbins, Roditi, Broughton, Parkinson, Weinberger, Hamill, Bartlett, Woodcock, M. Gibson, Gutierrez, Lockwood, and Morrow.

Hatlen, Burton, and Carroll F. Terrell, eds. *Kenneth Rexroth: Man and Poet* (University of Maine at Orono Press, forthcoming).

Work by Individual Authors

"Crystallization of American Poet and Japanese Calligrapher." *Tokyo Shimbun* (19 December 1955). In Japanese.

"Big Day for Bards at Bay." *Life*, Part 2 (9 September 1957): 105–8.

"Cool, Cool Bards." *Time* (2 December 1957): 71.

"Daddy-O." *New Yorker* (3 May 1958): 29–30.

"The Last Bohemian." *Time* (25 February 1966): 108. Review of *An Autobiographical Novel.*

"Rexroth, Kenneth." *Current Biography*, pp. 337–40. New York: Wilson, 1981.

"Rexroth, Kenneth." *Contemporary Authors*. Vol. 107, p. 428. Detroit: Gale, 1983.

"Kenneth Rexroth 1905–1982." *News & Letters* (July, 1982): 7.

Reviews of *In What Hour* in *Christian Century* (4 September 1940), *Oakland Tribune* (1 September 1940), *Columbus Dispatch* (15 September 1940), *Santa Barbara News* (29 September 1940), *Dallas Times-Herald* (6 October 1940), *Providence Journal* (3 November 1940), *New York Times* (23 February 1941).

Reviews of *An Autobiographical Novel* in *New York Times* (8 February 1966) 2, and (13 February 1966): VIII, 5.

Aaron, Daniel. *Writers on the Left: Episodes in American Literary Communism*, p. 341. New York: Harcourt, Brace, and World, 1961.

Aiken, Conrad. Review of *The Phoenix and the Tortoise* in article entitled, "Eberhart, Richard." *Collected Criticism*, pp. 168–70. London: Oxford, 1968. Reprint of *A Reviewer's ABC*, 1958.

Allsop, K. "Beaten." *Spectator* (13 March 1959): 350.

Andreae, Christina. "Marichiko Mon Amour White Cranes Green Rice." In *For Rexroth*, pp. 3–6.

Antler. "Rexroth As He Appeared to Exist." *Poetry Flash* 113 (August, 1982): 10. Reprinted in *Kyoto Review* 15 (Fall, 1982): 22. Poem.

Atlas, James. On *The Dragon and the Unicorn. London Magazine* (April–May, 1974).

Bartlett, Lee, ed. *The Beats: Essays in Criticism*, pp. 1, 2, 4, 43, 134, 149, 187–91. Jefferson, N. C.: McFarland, 1981.

―――. "Creating the Autochthon: Kenneth Rexroth, William Everson, and *The Residual Years." Sagetrieb* 2, no. 3 (Winter, 1983): 57–72.

Beach, Joseph Warren. *Obsessive Images: Symbolism in the Poetry of the 1930's and 1940's*, pp. 91, 241, 257–59, 286, 353–59. Minneapolis: University of Minnesota Press, 1960.

Bishop, John. Review of *One Hundred Poems from the Chinese*. *Comparative Literature* 10 (1958): 61–68.

Bly, Robert. *Talking All Morning*, pp. 22–23. Ann Arbor: University of Michigan Press, 1980.

Bogan, Louise. "Verse." *New Yorker* (9 May 1953): 121–22. Review of *The Dragon and the Unicorn*.

Broughton, James. "A Big Bang for Mr. Bangs." *Sagetrieb* 2, No. 3 (Winter, 1983): 33–36.

Bruchac, Joseph III. "On a Bare Branch." In *For Rexroth*, pp. 7–10.

Burdick, Eugene. "The Innocent Nihilists Adrift in Squaresville." *Reporter* (3 April 1958): 30–33.

Capouya, Emile. "Sad of Mind but Glad of Heart." *Saturday Review* (12 February 1966): 19–30. Review of *An Autobiographical Novel*.

Carruth, Hayden. "Our Best Nature Poet." Review of *The Heart's Garden, The Garden's Heart*. *Hudson Review* (Summer, 1968): 404.

Cassill, R. V. "Poetic Feast of Simplicity." *Chicago Sun-Times* (5 January 1964). Review of *Natural Numbers*.

Charters, Ann. *See* Miller, Brown.

Chung, Ling. "Kenneth Rexroth and Chinese Poetry: Translation, Imitation, and Adaptation." Ph.D. diss., University of Wisconsin, 1972.

———. "Forty Years in Between." In *For Rexroth*, pp. 11–13.

———. "Kenneth Rexroth's Renderings of Tu Fu's Poetry." *Rendition* (Chinese University of Hong Kong), 1985.

Ciani, Daniela. "Kenneth Rexroth: Poet of Nature and Culture." In *For Rexroth*, pp. 14–22. *See also* Daniela M. Ciani Forza.

Ciardi, John. "One for Rexroth." *In Fact*, p. 54. New Brunswick, N. J.: Rutgers University Press, 1962.

Clark, Tom. "Natural Wonders." *Rolling Stock* 9 (1985). Review of *The Selected Poems of Kenneth Rexroth*.

Cohn, Ruby. "Kenneth Rexroth." *Dialogue in American Drama*, pp. 263–65. Bloomington: Indiana University Press, 1971.

Dana, Robert. "An Interview with James Laughlin." *American Poetry Review* (November–December, 1981): 25–26.

Derleth, August. Review of *The Phoenix and the Tortoise*. *Voices* (Winter, 1945).

Dery, Mark. "The Lion Sleeps Tonight." *Poetry Flash* 113 (August, 1982): 3, 7.

Deutsch, Babette. *Poetry In Our Time*, pp. 24–25, 85, 91–92. New York: Columbia University Press, 1956.

DeVore, Lynn. "Rexroth, Kenneth." *Encyclopaedia of World Literature in the 20th Century*, rev. ed., vol. 4. Ed. Leonard·S. Klein. New York: Ungar, 1984, pp. 28–29.

Duncan, Robert. "On Kenneth Rexroth." Interviewed by Linda Hamalian. *Conjunctions* 4 (1983): 84–96.

Dunn, Douglas. "A Forgotten America." *Listener* (16 June 1977): 789–90. Review of *An Autobiographical Novel*.

Durnell, Hazel. *Japanese Cultural Influences on American Poetry and Drama*, pp. 132–38. Tokyo: Hokuseido, 1983.

Eberhart, Richard. Review of *The Signature of All Things. New York Times* (6 August 1950).

———. "A Voyage of the Spirit." Review of *The Dragon and the Unicorn. New York Times Book Review* (15 February 1953): 215.

———. "Poems of a Japanese Sojourn." *Nation* (22 April 1968). Review of *The Heart's Garden, The Garden's Heart*.

Eigner, Larry. Review of *The Dragon and the Unicorn. Black Mountain Review* (Summer, 1954): 49–57.

Eimerl, Sarel. "Compared with Me." *Reporter* (19 May 1966): 60, 62.

Eisenberg, Barry. "A Handful of Leaves." *Kuksu* (1975). Review of *New Poems*.

Ellmann, Richard and Robert O'Clair, eds. "Kenneth Rexroth." *Norton Anthology of Modern Poetry*, pp. 699–700; see also p. 14 and poems on pp. 700–705. New York: Norton, 1973.

Everson, William (Brother Antoninus). "Rexroth: Shaker and Maker." In *For Rexroth*, pp. 23–26.

———. "Afterword." In *The Beats: Essays in Criticism*, ed. Lee Bartlett, pp. 187–91.

———. "Everson on Rexroth: An Interview." Conducted by Linda Hamalian. *Literary Review* (Spring, 1983): 423–26.

Farrell, James T. *Studs Lonigan*, pp. 140–47. New York: Modern Library, 1938. Rexroth as Kenny.

Farwell, Beatrice. "Kenneth Rexroth: Life at the Cultural Frontier." *Gallery Notes*. Santa Barbara Museum of Art, July, 1981. With photograph of Rexroth by M. Gibson.

Ferlinghetti, Lawrence. "Horn on *Howl*." *Evergreen Review* 1, no. 4 (1957): 145–58.

———. "Special to *Poetry Flash*." *Poetry Flash* 113 (August, 1982): 8.

——. "A Tribute." In *Dictionary of Literary Biography Yearbook*. Detroit: Gale, 1982.

Ferril, Thomas Hornsby. Review of *The Signature of All Things*. *San Francisco Chronicle* (12 March 1950).

Fiedler, Leslie. Review of *An Autobiographical Novel*. *New York Herald Tribune* (6 March 1966): 10.

Fitts, Dudley. Review of *The Art of Worldly Wisdom*. *Saturday Review* 33 (17 September 1949): 220.

——. "A Poet Abroad." *New Republic* (9 February 1953): 19. Review of *The Dragon and the Unicorn*.

——. Untitled note in *New York Times Book Review*, Section 7 (23 July 1967): 8. Review of *Collected Shorter Poems*.

FitzGerald, William. "Twenty Years at Hard Labor." *Poetry* 57, no. 11 (November, 1940): 158–60. Review of *In What Hour*.

Flint, R. W. "Ambitious Venture." *Poetry* 78 (September, 1951): 356–60.

——. "Poets and Their Subjects." *New Republic* (18 February 1957): 19. Review of *In Defense of the Earth*.

Forza, Daniela M. Ciani. *Poesie de Kenneth Rexroth (1920–1956)*. Brescia, Italy: Paideia, 1982. *See also* Ciana, Daniela.

Foster, Richard. "With Great Passion, A Kind of Person." *Hudson Review* 13, no. 1 (Spring, 1960): 149–54. Review of *Bird in the Bush*.

——. "Lucubrations of an Outside Insider." *Minnesota Review* 3, no. 1 (Fall, 1962): 130–33. Review of *Assays*.

——. "The Voice of the Poet: Kenneth Rexroth." *Minnesota Review* 2, no. 3 (Spring, 1962): 377–84.

Fukuda, Rikutaro. *In the Shade of the West: Essays on Comparative Literature* (in Japanese), pp. 158–59. Tokyo: Elec, 1972.

Gardner, Geoffrey. "Editor's Introduction." In *For Rexroth*, pp. vii–xii.

——. "The Cast Snakeskin and the Uncut Stone." In *Kenneth Rexroth: Man and Poet*, Rexroth Festschrift. University of Maine at Orono Press, forthcoming.

Garren, Samuel Baity, "Quest for Value: A Study of the Collected Longer Poems of Kenneth Rexroth." Ph.D. diss., Louisiana State University, 1976.

Gibson, Keiko Matsui. "Kenneth Rexroth's Epiphany: June 6, 1982." *Kyoto Review* 16 (Spring, 1983): 16. Reprinted in *Kansai*

Time Out (Kobe, Japan, December, 1982): 23, and in *Vajradhattu Sun* (April–May, 1984): 19.

————— and Morgan Gibson. "Yosano Akiko." In *Critical Survey of Poetry: Foreign Series*, pp. 1713–19. Edited by Walton Beacham, La Canada, Calif.: Salem Press, 1984. On Rexroth's translations.

Gibson, Morgan. *Kenneth Rexroth.* New York: Twayne/G. K. Hall, United States Authors Series 208, 1972. Excerpted in "Kenneth Rexroth." *Contemporary Literary Criticism.* Ed. S. R. Runton and J. C. Stein. Vol. 22, pp. 343–48. Detroit: Gale Research Company, 1982. Also excerpted in *Poetry Flash* 113 (August, 1982): 8, and *A Library of Literary Criticism: Modern American Literature*, Vol. 4, pp. 402, 403. New York: Frederick Ungar Publishing Company, 1973.

————— and Hiroshi Murakami. *Tantric Poetry of Kūkai (Kōbō Daishi) Japan's Buddhist Saint.* Dedicated to Rexroth, with comment on Kūkai's influence on him. Ed. Montri Umavijani. Bangkok: Mahachula Buddhist University, 1982. Distributed by White Pine Press (Buffalo).

—————. "Kenneth Rexroth." In *Encyclopaedia of World Literature.* Ed. Wolfgang Bernard Fleischmann. Vol. 3, pp. 152–53. New York: Frederick Ungar Publishing Company, 1967.

—————. "Provincial Anarchy." *Kaleidoscope* (8–21 December 1967): 5, 12.

—————. Review of *The Burning Heart: Women Poets of Japan. Feminist Japan International Issue* 4 (Tokyo, February, 1978): 65.

—————. "Rexroth's Dharma." in *For Rexroth*, pp. 27–37. Also Gibson's poems for Rexroth reprinted, pp. 193–97, from *Speaking of Light*, Milwaukee: Morgan Press, 1979.

—————. "Kenneth Rexroth in Japan," *Kyoto Review* 15 (Kyoto, Fall, 1982): 23–28. Japanese translation by Keiko Matsui Gibson in *Seiza* (Tokyo, Fall, 1982): 36–39. English version excerpted in *Poetry Flash* 113 (August, 1982): 2, and in *Kansai Time Out* (Kobe, December, 1982): 22.

—————. "Kenneth Rexroth." In *Critical Survey of Poetry.* Ed. Walton Beacham, pp. 2348–55. La Canada, Calif.: Salem Press, 1982.

—————. "Rexroth." *New Pages* 2, no. 1 (Spring, 1982): 20. Reprinted in *Kyoto Review* 15 (Fall, 1982): 34–35. Reviews of *Excerpts from a Life* and *Conjunctions* 1. Reprinted in *Kyoto Review* 15 (Fall, 1982).

————. "Kenneth Rexroth: A Tribute." *Dictionary of Literary Biography Yearbook*. Ed. Matthew Bruccoli and Jean W. Ross, pp. 179–82. Detroit: Gale, 1982.

————. "Poetry Is Vision—Vision Is Love: Kenneth Rexroth's Philosophy of Literature." *Sagetrieb* 2, no. 3 (Winter, 1983): 85–100.

————. "Kaisetsu" (Comment). In *Kenneth Rexroth, Kokoro no Niwa*, edited and translated into Japanese by Katagiri, pp. 96–102.

————. "The Buddha-Mind of Kenneth Rexroth." *Vajradhattu Sun* (April–May, 1984): 19–20.

————. "The 'True-Word' of Kūkai and Modern Literature in English." *Mikkyo Bunka* (Reports on Esoteric Buddhism) 147 (September, 1984): 102–14. Reprinted in *The Nirvana of Kōbō Daishi: A 1150 Year Memorial*. Koya-san Monastery University, Japan, forthcoming.

————. "CA Interview" with Gibson on Rexroth conducted by Jean W. Ross, ed. *Contemporary Authors New Revision Series 14*, pp. 400–3. Detroit: Gale, 1985.

————. Review of *The Selected Poems of Kenneth Rexroth* (edited by Bradford Morrow). *American Poetry* 3, no. 2 (Winter, 1986): 86–89.

————. "Rexroth between Eros and Nirvana: on the Buddha's Way to *The Morning Star*." In *Kenneth Rexroth: Man and Poet*, forthcoming.

————. Review of Sanehide Kodama, *American Poetry and Japanese Culture. Comparative Literature Studies* (Spring, 1986): 85–90.

Gidlow, Elsa. "Random Memories of a Many-Faceted Friend." In *For Rexroth*, pp. 38–40.

Ginsberg, Allen and Ted Berrigan. "Kenneth Rexroth 1905–82." Unpublished and undated obituary for the American Academy and Institute of Arts and Sciences.

Golffing, Francis C. "Uncomfortable Humanism." *Poetry* 65 (February, 1945): 260–62.

————. See also J. R. Squires.

Goodman, Paul. Review of *The New British Poets. Poetry* 75, no. 4 (January, 1950): 239–40.

Gregory, Horace, and Marya Zaturenska. *A History of American Poetry 1900–1940*. New York: Harcourt, Brace and Company, 1946.

Griffin, Howard. Review of *The Signature of All Things*. *Saturday Review* (20 May 1950).

Grigsby, Gordon K. "The Presence of Reality: The Poetry of Kenneth Rexroth." *Antioch Review* 31, no. 3 (1971): 405–22.

Gutierrez, Donald. "Love Sacred and Profane: The Erotic Lyrics of Kenneth Rexroth." *Sagetrieb* 2, no. 3 (Winter, 1983): 101–12.

———. "Natural Supernaturalism: The Nature Poetry of Kenneth Rexroth." *Literary Review* (Spring, 1983): 405–22.

———. "Keeping an Eye on Nature: Kenneth Rexroth's Falling Leaves and Early Snow." *American Poetry* 1, no. 2 (Winter, 1984): 60–63.

Haines, John. "Homage to the Chinese." In *For Rexroth*, pp. 41–44.

Hall, Donald. "Kenneth Rexroth." *The Weather of Poetry*, pp. 3–11. Ann Arbor: University of Michigan Press, 1985. Reprinted from "Kenneth Rexroth and His Poetry," *New York Times Book Review* (23 November 1980): 9, 43, 44; and "Kenneth Rexroth" in *American Writing Today*. Vol 1. Forum Series (Voice of America Broadcasts). Washington, D. C.: United States International Communication Agency, 1982.

Hamalian, Linda. "On Kenneth Rexroth." Interview with Robert Duncan. *Conjunctions* 4 (1983): 84–96.

———. "Everson on Rexroth: An Interview." *Literary Review* (Spring, 1983): 423–26.

———. "The Road to Rexroth: A Study of The Homestead Called Damascus." Ph.D. diss., Temple University, 1983.

Hamill, Sam. "Requiem" (poem) and "Poetry and Jazz: A Memoir." *Sagetrieb* 2, no. 3 (Winter, 1983): 19–20, 53–56. The entire "Requiem" is in Hamill, *Fatal Pleasure*. Portland, Oreg.: Breitenbrush Publishers, 1984.

——— and Tree Swenson, eds. Untitled note. *Copperhead: A Giftbox for Kenneth Rexroth*. Port Townsend, Wash.: Copper Canyon Press, 1974.

Harrison, C. T. "Poems for an Ignorant Year." *Virginia Quarterly Review* 16 (October, 1940): 627–29. Review of *In What Hour*.

Hass, Robert. *Twentieth Century Pleasures: Prose on Poetry*, pp. 223–34. New York: Ecco Press, 1984.

Hassan, Ihab. *Contemporary American Literature 1945–1972: An Introduction*, pp. 93–94, 114, 119. New York: Frederick Ungar Publishing Company, 1973.

Hazard, James. "A Thin Valuable Look at Rexroth's Poetry." *Milwaukee Journal* (13 January 1985).

Hebb, Nancy. "Kenneth Rexroth." *Contemporary Authors New Revision Series 14*, pp. 393–99, 402–3. Detroit: Gale, 1985.

Howes, Victor. "Poetry of Moments." *Christian Science Monitor* (6 February 1980): 17.

Hu, Chung Ling. *See* Ling Chung.

Huerta, Father Alberto. "Jorge de Sena and Kenneth Rexroth: The Beat Generation." *Broteria* (in Portuguese, Lisbon, July, 1981), pp. 84–99.

————. *"In What Hour"* (unpublished eulogy read at Rexroth's funeral at Our Lady of Mount Carmel Church, Santa Barbara), 11 June 1982.

Humphries, Rolfe. "Too Much Abstraction." *New Republic* (12 August 1940): 221. Review of *In What Hour.*

Ignatow, David. Review of *The Signature of All Things. New Leader* (25 March 1950).

Jacobson, Dan. "America's 'Angry Young Men': How Rebellious Are the San Francisco Rebels?" *Commentary* 24 (December, 1957): 475–79.

Jaffe, Harold. *Christian Science Monitor* (11 July 1967): 9. Review of *Collected Shorter Poems.*

Jenkins, Joyce. "Rexroth at the San Francisco International Poetry Festival, 1980." *Poetry Flash* 113 (August, 1982): 9.

Kanaseki, Hisao. "Something about Rexroth" (in Japanese). *Seiza* (Fall, 1982): 16–18.

Katagiri, Yuzuru, ed. *See Kenneth Rexroth 1905–82.*

————, ed. and trans. *See Kenneth Rexroth yaku.*

————, ed. and trans. *See Kenneth Rexroth Hanawa.*

————, ed. and trans. *See Kenneth Rexroth Kokoro.*

————, "Kenneth Rexroth—'A Living Pearl'" and "About the Kenneth Rexroth Poetry Award" (in Japanese). *Seiza* (Fall, 1982): 50–55, 56–64.

Kazin, Alfred. "Father Rexroth and the Beats." *Reporter* 22 (3 March 1960): 54–56. Review of *Bird in the Bush.*

Kerouac, Jack. *The Dharma Bums.* New York: Signet Books, 1958. Rexroth as Reinhold Cacoethes.

Kirsch, Robert. "A Study of American Poetry." *Los Angeles Times* (9 July 1971). Review of *American Poetry in the Twentieth Century.*

————. "A Spiritual Home in Japan." *Los Angeles Times* (29 July 1977). Review of *The Buddhist Writings of Lafcadio Hearn*.

————. "Rexroth Bursts upon the '20's." *Los Angeles Times* (3 October 1978). Review of *An Autobiographical Novel*.

————. "On Kenneth Rexroth." In *For Rexroth*, pp. 45–46.

Koch, Vivienne. Review of *The Phoenix and the Tortoise*. *New York Herald Tribune* (14 January 1945).

Kodama, Sanehide. *American Poetry and Japanese Culture*. Hamden, Conn.: Archon Books, 1984.

————. "Bohemians in Search of Oriental Values: Kyoto and American Poets." *Rising Generation* 124, no. 9 (1 December 1978): 516–18.

————. "Kenneth Rexroth and Classical Japanese Poetry." *Kyoto Review* 15 (Fall, 1982): 6–19. Original version in *Annual Report of Studies*, pp. 180–201. Kyoto: Doshisha Women's College, 1978.

————. "Kenneth Rexroth and Japan." In *For Rexroth*, pp. 47–52.

————. Rexroth obituary (in Japanese) In *Kyoto Shimbum*, June, 1982.

————. "Rexroth and Women: In Search for the Eternal Figure of Marichi-ten: (in Japanese). *Seiza* (Fall, 1982): 30–35.

Kriegel, Leonard. "Rexroth: Citizen of Bohemia." *Nation* (6 June 1966): 688–89. Review of *An Autobiographical Novel*.

Kuo, Ta-Hsia. "Review of *Love and the Turning Year*: the Poetry of Kenneth Rexroth." *Antioch Review* 31, no. 3 (Fall, 1971): 153–55.

Laughlin, James. Interview conducted by Robert Dana. *American Poetry Review* (November, 1981): 19–30.

————. "A Tribute." *Dictionary of Literary Biography Yearbook*, p. 182. Detroit: Gale, 1982. Reprinted from *Poetry Pilot* (December, 1982).

————. "Remembering Kenneth Rexroth." *American Poetry Review* (January–February, 1983): 18.

————. "The Art of Publishing Part II." Interviewed by Richard Ziegfeld. *Paris Review* 90 (Winter, 1983): 112–60.

Lawler, Justus George. "Rexroth: A Personal Memoir." In *For Rexroth*, pp. 55–57.

Lee, Joseph E. Review of *One Hundred Poems from the Chinese*. *Literature East and West* 4, no. 4 (China Issue): 394–97.

Leonard, John. "Curmudgeons, Libel, Snobs, and Writing." *New York Times Book Review* (4 August 1980): 21.

Le Pellec, Yves. "Souvenirs de la Baie par Kenneth Rexroth." *Beat Generation.* Special issue of *Entretiens* (Paris, 1975): 155–62.

Lerner, Rachelle K. Ph.D. diss. in progress on Rexroth's cubism in painting and poetry, University of Toronto.

Levertov, Denise. "A Note on the Dedication." *Copperhead: A Gift for Kenneth Rexroth.* Port Townsend, Wash.: Copper Canyon Press, 1974.

Lieberman, Laurence. Review of *The Heart's Garden, The Garden's Heart. Poetry* (April, 1969).

Liebowicz, Herbert. *New York Times Book Review* (23 March 1975). Review of *New Poems.*

Lipton, Lawrence. *The Holy Barbarians.* New York: Julian Messmer, 1959.

———. "Notes toward an Understanding of Kenneth Rexroth with Special Attention to 'The Homestead Called Damascus.' *Quarterly Review of Literature* 9, no. 2 (1957): 37–46.

———. "The Poetry of Kenneth Rexroth." *Poetry* 40, no. 3 (June, 1957): 168–80.

———. "Rexroth." *Los Angeles Free Press* Part II (10 January 1969): 1, 22–23.

Lockwood, William J. "Toward a Reappraisal of Kenneth Rexroth: The Poems of His Middle and Late Periods." *Sagetrieb* 2, no. 3 (Winter, 1983): 113–34.

———. "Kenneth Rexroth's Versions of Li Ch'ing Chao." *Tamkang Review* (Winter, 1984).

———. "Kenneth Rexroth's Chicago Poems," unpublished.

Malkoff, Karl. "Poetry of Vision, Poetry of Action: *Southern Review* 6, no. 2 (Spring, 1970): 572–88.

McCarthy, Mary. *The Groves of Academe,* pp. 272–95. New York: Harcourt, Brace, 1952. Rexroth as Vincent Keogh.

McClure, Michael. "Planh." *Poetry Flash* 113 (August, 1982): 3. Reprinted in *Sagetrieb* 2, no. 3 (Winter, 1983): 26.

Meltzer, David. "Kenneth Rexroth. *The San Francisco Poets,* pp. 9–55. New York: Ballantine Books, 1971.

———. "KR." In *For Rexroth,* pp. 58–59.

———. "After the Interview." *Poetry Flash* 113 (August, 1982): 1, 10.

Merwin, W. S. "From a Letter." In *For Rexroth,* p. 60.

Miller, Brown, and Ann Charters. "Kenneth Rexroth." In *The Beats: Literary Bohemians in America*. Ed. Ann Charters. *Dictionary of Literary Biography*. Vol. 2, pp. 456–64. Detroit: Gale, 1983.

Miller, Henry. "Poems That Grow Like Flowers." *San Francisco Chronicle* (10 February 1957). Review of Chinese translations.

Mills, Ralph J. *Contemporary American Poetry*, pp. 26, 89, 179–80, 183, 239, 245, 254. New York: Random House, 1965.

———. *Cry of the Human: Essays on Contemporary American Poetry*, pp. 7, 16, 39, 248, 271. Urbana: University of Illinois Press, 1975.

———. "Recent Prose." *Poetry* 102, no. 4 (July, 1963): 270. Review of *Assays*.

Mitgang, Herbert. "When a Vagabond Artist Breaks the American Mold." *New York Times*, Section 4 (13 June 1982): 9.

Mittleman, Leslie B. "New Poems." Review in *Masterplots*, pp. 209–11. Ed. F. N. McGill. Englewood Cliffs, N. J.: Salem Press, 1974.

Montague, John. "American Pegasus." *Studies* 48 (Summer, 1959): 183–91.

Moorehouse, Frank. "The American Poet's Visit." *Sydney Southerly* 28 (Australia, 1968): 275–85.

Morrow, Bradford. Introduction to *Selected Poems* by Kenneth Rexroth, pp. ix–xxii. New York: New Directions, 1984.

———. "A Garland-Note for Kenneth Rexroth." In *For Rexroth*, pp. 61–62.

"To a Friend in Wake of a Ballyhoo" (poem) and "An Outline of Unpublished Rexroth Manuscripts, and an Introductory Note to Three Chapters from the Sequel to *An Autobiographical Novel*." *Sagetrieb* 2, no. 3 (Winter, 1983): 19–20, 135–46.

Mottram, Eric, ed. Introduction. *The Kenneth Rexroth Reader*. London: Cape, 1972.

Murray, Michelle. "Rexroth: Figure of Wisdom." *National Catholic Reporter* 7 (May, 1971): 13. Review of *With Eye and Ear*.

Nakayama, Yō. "Prescription for Being a Total Human Being: *An Autobiographical Novel* (1966)" (in Japanese). *Seiza* (Fall, 1982): 20–29.

Olson, Ray. "Paying Joyful Homage to the Polymath Poet." *In These Times* (6–12 May 1981): 19. Review of *For Rexroth*.

Parkinson, Thomas, ed. "Phenomenon or Generation?" *A Casebook on the Beat*. New York: Thomas Y. Crowell, 1961.

————. "Kenneth Rexroth, Poet." *Ohio Review* (Winter, 1976): 54–67.

————. "Reflections on Kenneth Rexroth." *Sagetrieb* 2, no. 3 (Winter, 1983): 37–44.

Perkins, David. *A History of Modern Poetry from the 1890's to the High Modernist Mode*, p. 410. Cambridge, Mass.: Harvard University Press, 1976.

Perloff, Marjorie. "Poetry and the Common Life." *Sulfur* 12 (1985): 160–64. Review of *Selected Poems*.

Podhoretz, Norman. "A Howl of Protest in San Francisco." *New Republic* (16 September 1957): 20.

Powell, Lawrence Clark. "In the Words of Kenneth Rexroth." *New York Times Book Review* (22 November 1964): 2.

Pritchard, William H. *Hudson Review* (Summer, 1967): 313. Review of *Collected Shorter Poems*.

Purcell, James Mark. "Kenneth Rexroth: Poetics, Populism, and the Chicago Kid." *Cresset* 36, no. 9 (September, 1973): 10–15.

Richards, Janet. *Common Soldiers*. San Francisco: Archer Press, 1979.

Robbins, Doren. "Tribute to Kenneth Rexroth: Poet Committing the Act of Magic." *Sagetrieb* 2, no. 3 (Winter, 1983): 29–31.

Roditi, Eduard. "Letter to Kenneth Rexroth." *Sagetrieb* 2, no. 3 (Winter, 1983): 32. Poem.

Rodman, Selden. "Gnomic, Fastidious Verses." *New York Herald Tribune* (7 May 1950). Review of *The Signature of All Things*.

Rosenthal, M. L. "Outside the Academy." *The Modern Poets*, pp. 155–56. New York: Oxford University Press, 1960.

————. "Rexroth: The Fact and the Fury." *Nation* (28 September 1957): 199–200.

Ross, Jean. "CA Interview" with Morgan Gibson on Rexroth. *Contemporary Authors New Revision Series 14*, pp. 400–403. Detroit: Gale, 1985.

Rothenberg, Jerome. *The Revolution of the Word: A New Gathering of American Avant Garde Poetry, 1914–1945*. New York: Continuum, 1974.

Rukeyser, Muriel. "Lyrical 'Rage.'" *Saturday Review* (9 November 1957): 15. Review of *In Defense of the Earth*.

Safdie, Joe. Untitled Note. *Poetry Flash* 113 (August, 1982): 9.

Sakurai, Emiko. "The Oriental Tradition in the Poetry of Kenneth Rexroth." Ph.D. diss., University of Alabama, 1973.

————. "Kenneth Rexroth." *World Literature Today* 52, no. 1 (Winter, 1978). Review of Japanese translations.

————. "The Noh Plays of Kenneth Rexroth: A Study of the Fusion of Classical Greek and Japanese Traditions." In *For Rexroth*, pp. 63–80.

Sanchez, Thomas. "Rexroth—A Dream in a Cavernous Sea." *Los Angeles Times Book Review* (20 June 1982): 6.

Scott, Winfield Townley. "*The Dragon and the Unicorn*." *New York Herald Tribune* (1 February 1953): 8.

Shapiro, Karl. "Passport-Carrying Member of the Academy." *Los Angeles Times Book Review* (24 January 1971): 10, 12. Review of *With Eye and Ear*.

Shearer, Lois. "Time Will Care for Rexroth." *San Francisco Sunday Examiner-Chronicle* (27 June 1982): 3.

Shiffert, Edith. "In Memoriam for Kenneth Rexroth, Santa Barbara." *Kyoto Review* 15 (Fall, 1982): 20–21.

————. "After the Vacancy of Darkness." In *For Rexroth*, pp. 353–54.

Shiraishi, Kazuko. "Kenneth Rexroth." In *For Rexroth*, p. 81.

————. "Memorial Tribute for Kenneth Rexroth" (in Japanese). *Will* 4 (Tokyo, Autumn, 1982): 30–38.

Snyder, Gary. "Kenneth Rexroth." *Kyoto Review* 15 (Fall, 1982): 2. Japanese translation in *Seiza* (Fall, 1982): 19.

Solt, John. "For KR." *Kyoto Review* 15 (Fall, 1982): 2.

————. Poems in *For Rexroth*, pp. 335–61.

Sorrentino, Gil. "Good House." *Poetry* 104 (June, 1964): 179–81. Review of *Natural Numbers*.

Spector, Robert D. *Saturday Review* (15 March 1969): 33. Review of *Collected Longer Poems*.

Spiller, Robert E., gen. ed. *A Literary History of the United States*, pp. 1430–31, 1484. New York: Macmillan, 1974.

Squires, J.R. and Francis Golffing. "Two Views of Rexroth." *Poetry* 76 (June, 1950): 156–61.

Stafford, William. "A Five Book Shelf." *Poetry* 109 (December, 1967): 184–88. Review of *Collected Shorter Poems*.

Stepanchev, Stephen. "Triumph of the Particular." *New Leader* (24 April 1968): 20–21. Review of *Collected Shorter Poems*.

Steuding, Bob. *Gary Snyder*, pp. 19, 22, 45, 110–15, 119–24, 161, 167. Boston: Twayne/G. K. Hall, 1976.

Stewart, Dean. "Rexroth: A Sextant of Experience from an Inside Outsider." *Los Angeles Times* (3 August 1980): 3.

Stock, Robert. "The Hazards of Art." *Nation* (24 March 1969): 378. Review of *Collected Longer Poems*.

Symons, Julian. "The Education of an American." *Times Literary Supplement* (25 March 1977): 332. Review of *An Autobiographical Novel*.

Taguchi, Tetsuya. "Recollection of Kenneth Rexroth." *English Friends Association Bulletin* (*Naru*) 15 (Kochi University, Japan: Winter, 1983): 27–29.

Tarn, Nathaniel. "The White Widow." *Sagetrieb* 2, no. 3 (Winter, 1983): 27–28. Poem.

Tinker, Carol. "The Well Field," In *For Rexroth*, pp. 127–29. Poem.

———. "Poem on a Photograph of Kenneth Rexroth by Elizabeth Burstein." *Sagetrieb* 2, no. 3 (Winter, 1983): 18.

Unterecker, John. "Calling the Heart to Order." *New York Times Book Review* (23 July 1967): 8. Review of *Collected Shorter Poems*.

Van Ghent, Dorothe Bendon. Introduction and "Kenneth Rexroth" (Chapter 5). "Some Problems of Communication," pp. 1–15, 94–123. Master's thesis, Mills College, 1935.

Wagenknecht, Edward. "4 American Writers" (Review of Gibson, *Kenneth Rexroth*, and books on other writers). *News-Tribune* (23 February 1973).

Wagner, Linda. Review of *Kenneth Rexroth*. "Poetry: the 1930's to the Present." *American Literary Scholarship*. Ed. J. Albert Robbins, p. 340. Durham, N. C.: Duke University Press, 1974.

Weinberger, Eliot. "Kenneth Rexroth 1905–1982." *Sulfur* 5 (1982): 4–6.

———. "At the Death of Kenneth Rexroth." *Sagetrieb* 2, no. 3 (Winter, 1983): 45–52.

West, Hollie I. "'Old Beat' Rexroth: Poetry, Anarchy and Oriental Detachment." *Washington Post* (19 December 1976): 1, 4.

Williams, Jonathan. Interview by Ronald Johnson. *Conjunctions* 7 (1985): 229, 233–34.

Williams, William Carlos. "Verse with a Jolt to It." *New York Times Book Review* (28 January 1951): 5. Review of *Beyond the Mountains*.

—————. "Letter to Marianne Moore." *The Selected Letters of William Carlos Williams.* Ed. John C. Thirwall. New York: McDowell, Obilensky, 1957. Comment on *The Dragon and the Unicorn.*

—————. "Two New Books by Kenneth Rexroth." *Poetry* 90 (June, 1957): 180–90. Reviews of *In Defense of the Earth* and *One Hundred Poems from the Chinese.*

Wilson, Bryan. "The Communer Belt." *New Statesman* (2 January 1976): 18. Review of *Communalism.*

Woodcock, George. "A Rexroth Retrospective." *New Leader* (17 February 1969): 21–23.

—————. "Bohemian Half-Worlds." *New Leader* (21 September 1970): 19–20. Review of *The Alternative Society.*

—————. "Realms beyond the Mountains." In *For Rexroth*, pp. 82–94. Review of *Beyond the Mountains.*

—————. "Rage and Serenity: The Poetic Politics of Kenneth Rexroth." *Sagetrieb* 2, no. 3 (Winter, 1983): 73–84.

Wright, James. "From a Letter." In *For Rexroth*, p. 95.

Yaguchi, Yorifumi. "The Poetry World of Kenneth Rexroth." *Seiza* (Fall, 1982): 40–49.

—————. *One Dimension of Modern American Poetry* (in Japanese), pp. 72–78. Tokyo: Oshisha, 1983.

Yglesias, Luis Ellicott. "Kenneth Rexroth and the Breakthrough into Life." In *For Rexroth*, pp. 96–110.

Index